MIND MATTERS

Mind Matters

Selected Papers of Ernest Kafka

Ernest Kafka

IPBOOKS.net
International Psychoanalytic Books

International Psychoanalytic Books (IPBooks)
New York • http://www.IPBooks.net

Mind Matters – Selected Papers of Ernest Kafka

Published by IPBooks, Queens, NY
Online at: www.IPBooks.net

Cover Image: Photo of Stubbs by Ernest Kafka

ISBN: 978-1-956864-01-4

To Heinz Hartmann

Table of Contents

CHAPTER 1

Illusion and Disillusion

(1997). *Journal of Clinical Psychoanalysis,* 6(1):55–77 Infantile Wishes: Fulfilled and Unfulfilled: Illusion and Disillusion. The A. A. Brill Lecture presented at the New York Psychoanalytic Society, November 29, 1994.

The expectation of pleasure to come is pleasurable itself. In childhood, unconscious expectations arise that childhood wishes will be satisfied in the future. These expectations persist and come to coexist with more realistic expectations of satisfaction. Thus, an illusory aspect enters into plans for and anticipations about the future. Analytic work requires that such illusory elements be revealed and modified. The fear of loss of the pleasure that lies in anticipating that illusions will be gratified in the future, impedes revision of childhood theories during development and motivates resistance in analysis. To deal with illusions tactfully is a technical challenge because deprivation of the satisfactions attending them is painful. This subject merits more emphasis than it has received.

Clinical work and general observation both lead to the conclusion that individuals accommodate to the changing contexts in which they exist, and make efforts to cause these contexts to accommodate to their desires. It seems to be a fairly general conclusion among analysts and nonanalysts alike, that desire, bodily and mental physiologic maturation, and developmental events all influence the evolution of conscious and unconscious perceptions and ideas throughout the course of life.

The unique history of a sociobiopsychologic person (Reiser, 1986) influences the contemporary organization of that person's interrelationship with the social context, both the broader context, and the narrower, clinically useful, transference context. Humans continue to have experiences that influence them to learn and to change their concepts and perceptions about their interrelationships with their environment, and these changes influence their future interrelationships. The present becomes the past that influences the future. The therapeutic analytic experience is one among a number of experiences that can bring about changes in perceptions, in ideas, and significantly, in ideas involving anticipatory judgments about potential unpleasure and pleasure.

Such changes alter the degree to which the inner world of fears and hopes resembles the actual world of dangers and satisfying possibilities. By and large, inner, psychic reality differs more from outer reality in children than it does in adults. At any age, inner and outer reality differ more in more pathological aspects of mental functioning than in less pathological ones, as seen by a relatively objective observer. "Oh wad som Power the giftie gie us to see oursel's as others see us," wrote Burns (1786).

During development, modification of one's subjective view of reality in a more realistic direction has a positive effect on adaptation. A more realistic view of reality enhances future gratification and diminishes future frustration, and may be considered a measure of mental health.

One aspect of the analytic work is to show the patient the origins and historical and current uses and benefits of transferences. Another is to help the patient see that transferences are literally transferred. They reflect incompletely revised theories and perceptions, which persist despite maturational and contextual change. Such unmodified arrangements are less likely to achieve adaptive intentions than revised arrangements that take account of changes in the subject and the subject's context. Therefore the patient benefits by better understanding the origins of his ideas and perceptions, their evolution and development, and the conscious and unconscious reasons why modifications of his ideas and perceptions have not kept pace with changes in his capacities and contexts.

At times, an analyst's interventions can foster contradictory views of the patient's relationship to the analyst, some reflecting his more subjective perceptions of the analytic relationship, and others reflecting more objective views. Usually, one or another of these views seems more correct to the patient, seems to correspond more accurately to "reality." But in such instances the patient often has a further, sometimes quite powerful reaction of discomfort, anger, and rejection of the intervention and/or of the analyst.

Forgetting, intellectual disavowal, resentment, flight to health, and interruption of treatment are among the negative responses to perceptions that include feelings of uncertainty and displeasure. They represent challenges to the analyst's understanding and tact. Sometimes, on the beneficial side, such situations lead to change in the balance between patients' tendencies to remain unchanged and the tendencies to adapt to a new context.

The tendency people have to remain as they are by avoiding any revision of their views of their relationships with the world, is of particular interest to the analyst, since patients' failure to revise views and construct new adaptations in changed circumstances, results in maintenance of unsatisfying, and often, destructive and self-destructive situations.

Why, we and patients ask, don't patients get better faster? A number of general theoretical ideas have been presented to answer this question. Kohut's idea, failure to form structure, Freud's death instinct, the resistance of the id, weakness of the ego, negative therapeutic reaction, narcissistic vulnerability, and propositions about limitations in inherent capacities to change are among such ideas. There have also been many clinical descriptions of individuals' idiosyncratic developments, and the influences that oppose change like vicissitudes of guilt, the consequences of trauma, overstimulation, and others.

I propose that the mind harbors conscious and unconscious fears of losing the gratifications that attend conscious and unconscious illusory anticipations that the future will provide satisfaction of childhood wishes, on the model of "when I, grown up, then." Such fears play an important part in motivating patients' tendencies to avoid change, and represent a particular clinical challenge and opportunity.

Analysis presents patients with an agreeable idea, that their childhood wishes can achieve symbolic, attenuated gratification. It also presents a disagreeable confrontation. They will never be able to satisfy childhood wishes except symbolically, in attenuated ways. Some of the pleasure in play, dreams, daydreams, and unconscious fantasies is the pleasure in the idea that the wished-for gratification, currently supported by perceptual elements, is currently actual. Another pleasure is in the comforting idea that wishes embodied in play, daydreams, and unconscious fantasies will become actualized in reality one day. In playing and dreaming, people use illusions to help achieve concurrent satisfaction. The pleasurable anticipation of future satisfaction is also partly dependent on illusion. Freud (1917) observed that man's "*naive* self-love" was wounded when he was deprived of his belief that the earth is at the center of the universe by the Copernican revolution, that he "occupies a privileged place in creation" by the Darwinian, and that "the ego is... master in its own house" by the Freudian psychological researches. My footnote adds another wounding blow, that the future holds no prospect of reversing

4

the deprivations attending these injuries to "human megalomania." Future gratification must be incomplete.

This disappointment is akin to narcissistic mortification, but differs insofar as it refers to hoped for future gratification of unsatisfied childhood wishes rather than to interference with current grandiosity (as described recently by Rothstein, 1991).

Patients resist disruption of illusions. Such resistance reflects fear of the loss of illusions about the prospects for future gratification of childhood wishes. Such fear should be added to the traditional list of fears of loss as a motivator of defense and resistance, and as an enemy of adaptation.

The following case reports are intended to illustrate some painful, but eventually, beneficial consequences of following the model for which I argue. This model suggests that we continue to remember that anxiety reflects anticipations of loss of objects, of object love, and of castration and superego disapproval, and motivates resistance. I focus on the idea that to some degree, all of us also resist accepting that gratifying illusions about the future are illusions. All children must endure frustration of many wishes, and they play, fantasize, and daydream about gratifying these wishes in the future. In some patients, to protect such pleasurable anticipation of future gratification is particularly important, and acts to impel resistance, to impede revising views, and to limit adaptive improvement.

Second, the illustrations underline the fact that analysts' comments that threaten such illusions can cause pain to the patient, that analytic change can involve significant distress as the illusory anticipatory satisfactions are diminished, as "shrinking" takes place. The negative reactions described below require explanations that specify these intermediate steps in the evolution of patients' responses to interventions.

SOME EXAMPLES OF CLINICAL PROBLEMS

On the advice of a previous therapist and at the insistence of his girlfriend who threatened to drop him unless he modified his drinking and drug taking, a 32-year-old man reluctantly sought consultation. According to him, his career was his problem. He was a playwright whose work was not read, produced, or appreciated. The community failed to appreciate his genius, his competitors envied him, and the "fact is," said he, "every success comes as a consequence of connections and salesmanship," which he lacked, derided, and eschewed. If he had a problem, it was that his anger and disappointment sometimes made it difficult to work.

Over the course of treatment, the following became evident: His plays tended to be arcane and unapproachable. Besides being confusing, they attacked and derided the audience to which he claimed he wanted to speak. He submitted material to producers with the attitude that his submission was a submission to their likely sadistic mistreatment. His response to those who encouraged him was to escalate demands on them, and to deluge them with material, less and less appropriate to their interests, and resembling less and less what they had originally liked.

These behaviors were motivated by desires to avoid the potential disappointment that failure might bring. They also gratified the patient's hostile, vengeful wishes, his guilty needs for punishment, his receptive and masochistic wishes, and, moreover, helped him maintain his grandiose sense of his importance. As might be expected, years of analytic work focused on these factors.

His parallel negative and provocative attitudes toward his girlfriend (later his wife), toward the analyst, friends, and others, also underwent extensive and repeated examination. This work produced memories of childhood frustrations and disappointments that concerned his relationship with his seductive, mean, and withholding mother who was alcoholic, his aloof, egocentric, and depreciating father, his response to the birth and development of a younger sibling, to defeats and embarrassments at school, to his unsatisfactory relationships with teachers, with his previous therapist and with the analyst.

The main emphases, early on, were, first, on how he defended himself against anticipations of humiliation, and against imagined retaliation in response to his angry wishes and to the provocations to which they gave rise, second, on his guilty self-punishing feelings, which caused him to feel undeserving and helped to make him unrewarded and unappreciated, and third, on his homosexual, receptive, and masochistic hopes. The occasions that allowed discussion of this kind early in the analysis, were mainly experiences of disappointment in current life, both as they came about as a result of unprovoked incidents—deaths, illnesses, separations, for example—and as they came about as a consequence of provocations by the patient.

Rather clear behavioral change, and enhanced gratification in life took place over a course of years. The patient married, had children, gave up drink and drugs, and became a more integrated member of his social community. The power of his need to see himself as superhuman and invulnerable, to reject, torture, tease, and humiliate others, and to experience humiliation himself lessened.

Nevertheless, these remained important, despite his increasing awareness that his attitudes and their behavioral manifestations expressed needs to master, undo, and reverse earlier experiences of weakness, and also caused him to feel guilty and rejected. He knew he expressed hostility and contempt, and thus reaped the punishment he feared. He also knew much about how this pattern had come about and what functions it served. His underlying grandiose wishes to be self-sufficient, and hermaphroditic, and also his wishes to win his parents' love, while punishing them for what he had suffered, became more defined. He hoped to hit a home run, to write a huge hit, to be discovered and appreciated, to revel in the humiliation of the community that would be punished by being forced to admit how wrong it had been about his genius.

These wishes had both grandiose narcissistic aspects, and also, typical "neurotic" childhood wishful aspects. The expectation that they would be gratified in the future was an unchanged aspect of the patient's mental life. Enactments that involve behavior such as childhood exhibitionistic, provocative behavior such as soiling in school, designed to embarrass his parents, while gaining him a reputation as a remarkable bad boy; adolescent poetizing praise of de Sade and equating of Attila the Hun with Albert Schweitzer; and early adult drunken fighting, which he then proclaimed was artistic creativity, as everyone would eventually recognize.

A change in focus attended the changes in the patient. The patient's increased investment in practical social life led him to try to make more realistic efforts to be appreciated by behaving in a way that would please others, and his pleasures in doing so also increased. This tendency was apparent in his attitudes about his children, wife, and work. However, there were interferences; he could not maintain what he now regarded as behavior likely to lead to a practically satisfying result.

Now it became evident to me, and I made it so to the patient, that though he still feared making efforts because of anticipations of humiliating failure, because of projections of guilty punishment fantasies over his unexpressed hostility and its expressed derivative forms, and because of his need to satisfy receptive wishes, yet, he had become more able to do so, and had had some successes.

However, successes gave him only transient satisfaction. Successes, rather than making it easier for him to continue making active efforts to achieve the pleasures he wanted, seemed to have the contrary effect of making it harder. When people responded favorably to his work, he became angry, depressed, off-putting, reluctant to revise his work, and he had no new ideas. When his wife responded positively to his more friendly advances, he withdrew from her, and reverted to his previous overbearing and uncaring manner.

Once it had been rejection; now it was success that was followed by disappointment, anger, and feelings of rejection and unjust mistreatment. "How can so-and-so be a success when I am not," was again a frequently asked question, as was an associated idea that people who were more psychopathic and less feelingful, who could get away with cruelty, self-promotion, and unconcern had more satisfaction than he. Again, he tried to demonstrate the activity of cliques that were against him, and to show he was independent and self-sufficient, did not care what anyone thought, indeed, was filled with contempt for others, was invulnerable and superhuman. Now the grandiosity was softer and more transient than it had been earlier. I told the patients all of this, and he became annoyed with me. He changed the subject, became angry and critical of me, and complained that I failed to appreciate him.

Repeated instances occurred where he avoided some project, gradually lost his reluctance, carried it out, and received a positive response, and then reacted negatively. Eventually, the patient accepted that both failure and disappointment, and accomplishment, success, and gratification seemed to be followed by similar effects. He responded to both failure and success with anger and rebelliousness, with some degree of grandiosity, and in the analysis, by becoming obtuse, belittling, rejecting, and provocative.

Mr. A gradually came to understand his wishes to be dominating, that he experienced human contact as a threat to his sense of control and superiority and, sadly and angrily, he gradually, partially accepted that he fell far short of evidencing the greatness he continued to believe was in him. However, he expected that this potential greatness would ultimately appear and be recognized.

I pointed out how gratifying his idea was that he would eventually be recognized as a genius, and that then he would be free to express all his resentment, and take his revenge for the sufferings he had felt in the past. The patient became very angry that I termed this an idea: It was an expectation, not an idea.

He stopped working, became sexually aloof from his wife, and showed increased provocativeness. I noted that this response failed to take into account the useful analytic work in which he was engaged. The cherished illusion that his wishes could eventually be satisfied by a home run might be satisfying now, but, as he had noted, he repeatedly suffered because nothing in actuality lived up to his expectations. The result, instead, was that he often felt angry, vindictive, and disappointed, behaved destructively and self-destructively, and missed out on many pleasures that would be available if he allowed himself to accept more in actuality, even at the price of sacrificing some pleasure in the expectation of satisfying his childhood wishes in the future.

The following instance is an example of several I might relate that made it possible for the patient to see that he reacted more positively to deprivation than to gratification, because satisfaction meant accepting limitations, and giving up the pleasant illusion that he might have everything in the end.

At a reading of his work he wanted to show up his father by demonstrating that he was capable of achieving fame and admiration. The audience represented his mother, whom he wanted to win. His father would be abashed and humiliated. Other means planned to accomplish this end, included, being a better father and therefore, having better children, and also, entering into a social world unavailable to his father. In this instance, his work gained him praise, and his father seemed both pleased and a bit abashed. The patient's initial pleasure was short lived. He began to feel angry and morose. What was a bit of success? It hardly added up to much after so many previous disappointments. Was this all there was? Wasn't he entitled to more? Weren't others more successful and more fortunate? Besides, perhaps he was undeserving. It was a mistake to have obvious success. Others would feel angry and vengeful. How well he knew those feelings.

He might be in danger. After all, it was easy for him to be an artist. His father's money provided him the means, the time, the office. He hadn't accomplished that much on his own. On the other hand, others, inferior to him were better appreciated, because they were better connected, or belonged to a privileged group, like women and the homeless. The sequence was, anxious anticipation before the performance, performance, brief satisfaction, disappointment, envy, and anger, guilt and fear, and provocative rationalization in feeling victimized.

Like Freud on the Acropolis, and like others whose accomplishments are followed by anxious, let-down states, the patient was wrecked by success, a criminal from the sense of guilt, and an exception (Freud, 1916). That is, the analysis revealed that his success carried with it ideas of increasing power, the belief in the possibility that he might carry out his destructive wishes in reality, guilt over his rivalrous, sadistic, vengeful inclinations, fear of being exposed to others who might gang up on him, renewed attempts to feel safer by becoming more childlike, and renewed attempts to feel victimized and exceptional in order to deserve rewards.

Discussion of these points included making connections with historically earlier variants, like his wrecking his relationships with women who found him appealing in his teens, or like his withdrawal from friendships earlier, or like his oafish exaggeration of his messiness in a form of self-mockery that also especially mocked his father, and gave rise to punishment by him. This resulted in some easing of the intensity of this response to experiences of ability and satisfaction. As the guilty, provocative, and self-destructive side of his responses to success diminished, the more depressive elements became more apparent. It seemed that every experience of capacity carried with it, an experience of limited capacity.

Again, the patient noted that as these matters were better understood, his work seemed to be changing. It was better received, partly because viewers found it more direct and approachable. Apparently, the withholding of the work, the avoidance of showing, had influenced the work itself, limiting its accessibility when it was shown. The patient wanted not to be separated from his work, not to give up possessing it exclusively, and controlling it. He tended to treat it as he did his friends, children, younger sibling, and wife.

To consider termination was difficult for Mr. A. When I took one of his references to ending the analysis seriously, the patient's reactions were, as expectable, various and intense: anger intensified. In addition to the feelings of increased resentment that I was willing to let him go, and the connections with earlier deprivations and fears of abandonment on many levels, and the fear of punishment and loss, and the need for self-punishment, expiation, and denial of his wishes, he also discovered a sense of impending loss of an important illusion.

He now realized that he had believed that seeing me maintained me, his money took care of me, I needed to be stimulated by his difficult problems. He kept me alive, he possessed the power to create important writing, and more. He maintained my life, and the lives of his family. I was the mother who truly depended on him, with whom he was necessary, in control, and successful. I would always be with him, accepting his love and hatred. As long as nothing interfered with his inner conviction that these illusions were truths, and that

12

the satisfaction they provided him would continue, he was relatively content.

My willingness to let him go meant he was not, and would not become the needed, generative, bisexual, creative being, he wished to be. This set of ideas was an important element in his wish not to finish the analysis, and not to finish, show, or see his work produced, and not to finish being a child in various aspects of his perceptions and behaviors. He had laboriously built up the idea of his eventual glory, and the shrinkage this notion was undergoing as he gradually came to accept that he was human, vulnerable, and finite, was painful.

One day the patient said he had seen the film, *The Unforgiven*. Clint Eastwood had said, to a younger man who realized killing someone was a terrible thing, "You take away everything a man has and everything he hopes for." The analysis had killed him, the patient said, because it had deprived him of his hopes. The next day, the patient tried to identify a tune that kept going through his head. It turned out to be a Peggy Lee song, "Is That All There Is," a song of repeated disappointed illusions.

This lengthy analysis demonstrated that the patient had developed characteristics intended to control and express a number of antisocial, sadistic traits based on his many wounding, humiliating experiences at the hands of his parents. These characteristics also reflected compensating grandiose narcissistic (Freud's "megalomanic") illusions. He wanted to inflict pain on others and be impervious to it himself. He wanted to be self-created, a hermaphrodite who gave birth independent of all outside influence. He wanted to be an Attila and a Picasso, to be loved without giving pleasure. His work inhibitions were consequent to fears of abandonment and punishment because of the sadistic and masochistic aspects of his acts, and also, to his unconscious anticipations of being disappointed in the results, no matter what. Seemingly good results were disappointing because they failed to produce the grand results that would have gratified his childhood wishes, and deprived him of the pleasure in anticipating. Analysis confronted him with the inevitable: his childhood wishes would never be completely gratified. Suffering and negative responses, "regressions" occurred repeatedly in response to such disappointments, but revision of his thinking and in the illusions he harbored did take place. The patient became more realistic, and in some ways, more satisfied.

ANOTHER CASE

A woman in her forties came with feelings of anger and depression that were triggered by the revelation that her boss and mentor had been revealed as an embezzler, and had fled the country. She thought that disillusionment about this man to whom she had devoted herself in a servile way for years, had caused her feelings of sadness, resentment, listlessness, and lack of interest in continuing in her work.

It seemed she also took a similar protective, self-abnegating attitude toward her children, who were now grown, one at college and the second, soon to go, and towards her husband. This latter was a very accomplished and successful professional whom she greatly respected, loved, and admired, but whom she also regarded, and treated as though he was a quite needy, dependent person. She claimed she had to advise him about all the decisions he made, whether in business or personal life, to provide him with friends and entertainment, and to initiate sexual activity, often with the sacrifice of her own gratification.

She took a similar view of her relationship to her (apparently) rather independent children. The son who was away at college seemed to be doing well. Yet she sent him packages containing food or clothing, discussed his activities with him daily, advised him

14

about his friendships, and was generally, and in her view, necessarily, involved with many aspects of his life. The second child, who had required special educational attention earlier because of a reading difficulty, had apparently surmounted this, as well as a severe illness that had required several hospitalizations during childhood, and was also doing well.

She presented a view of herself as feeling obligated to take care of other people, guilty when she failed to get their approval and appreciation, and exploited by them.

Her history revealed that her parents had divorced when she was 5 and her only sister 3. Her mother, with whom she lived for a year after the divorce, had then remarried and left the country. Subsequently she and her sister lived with her father. He involved himself with a succession of women, and remarried soon after the patient's sister went away to college. At college, the patient met her husband, and after a courtship of some months they married.

In treatment she initially seemed cooperative. Her depressive feelings disappeared in a few weeks, during which she spoke about her history and about the events of her current life at length. As a summer break neared, she began to think that treatment was not really indicated, that she had nothing further to talk about, that I had not been of much help to her, that she really had no problems. At the same time, she began to express feelings of resentment about her subservient attitude toward the men in her life, me included. Why did she have to be the one to be the assistant, the good girl, the one who looked after her father and her superior at work?

I expressed curiosity about the fact that this feeling of having had to submit, or at least, of having submitted, was coming up near the time of our vacation separation. Perhaps her self-deprecating, subservient attitude was a way of coping with disappointment. The patient responded feelingfully, describing her disappointment when her father remarried, and when the boss absconded. She said she assumed that she had formed some attachment to me that was responsible for her feelings of irritation about the separation about to occur. She thus identified feelings of anger resulting from the disappointment of loss.

In the next year, the patient revealed more of the less rosy side of her early life. She talked about her loneliness after her mother left, and about how difficult it was to have to make her own way without a more understanding parent than her father could be. She described difficulties she had had dealing with her own learning disorder, now revealed to me for the first time. She spoke of having been sent away to a strange, and to her, forbidding boarding school in her early teens, a historical element she had elided before. As we discussed these matters, the patient became more resentful about having had to grow up quickly and on her own. Some constructions about how she might have felt at the time of her sister's birth when she was 3 led to some researches on her part.

These revealed that she had indeed suffered at that time. She had been enuretic and withdrawn, and going to prekindergarten, which had coincided more or less with the sister's birth, which had been difficult for her. This revelation led to some discussion about how disappointment and anger had complicated her control problems, and about how important it had become for her to be in control of her resentment, as well as of her body. These factors were discussed as factors leading to her passive, masochistic, seemingly dependent attitude.

In the third analytic year, the patient became more angry, ostensibly about the role of helpful daughter / older sister, devoted to the interests of others, which she thought she had been assigned. She came to resent the routine of the analytic work, and leaving came up again. Her manner with me was occasionally contemptuous and provocative. Interpretations pointed out that disappointments stimulated her anger, and that provocative self-punishing behavior then followed. However, the anger persisted despite her method of directing it against herself, and she now sought to explain it by the theory that subservience had been imposed on her, and she was rebellious about the subservience, which actually was, by now, an independent self-protective characteristic.

Concurrently, her husband needed to make some career decisions. His opinion about what he should do differed from hers. She thought he should stay in his current, secure, and profitable position, but he decided to enter into a partnership with a colleague, and set up a new enterprise. She seemed quite angry, and disappointed at this decision, and was worried for her husband. "Suppose he fails," was the idea. He might be being too impulsive. I presented the idea that, having suffered because of childhood losses, and because of body control difficulties, and given how anger had been stimulated by these circumstances, she now wanted to control her husband as a representative of herself, and as a way of expressing her anger. Meanwhile, the patient continued to talk of the relationship with the superior who ran off. She had concerns about me as well. I seemed a bit listless. Was I perhaps not well?

I said she complained about having to submerge her interests to take care of needy men who never appreciated her enough. On the other hand, she had told me how capable her husband was, and that he had looked forward to running his own enterprise for some time. Had she not complained about being subservient and wanting more independence for herself, and might not her husband have similar desires? Finally, I suggested that the feeling of responsibility for her husband and former superior, and particularly for me, seemed to contain some element of domineering wishes, and fears that she might have insufficient control of them.

At this, the patient became quite irate. She lost her temper quite dramatically, told me I was insensitive and hostile, and left the session. It took some days for her to become less angry and accusing. She still felt my idea threatened her, and took something important away from her. Evidently her complaints about being used, while understandable in terms of her past history, concealed the fact that this position was very dear to her, and not only because it satisfied receptive, masochistic, and guilty wishes, and maintained a sense of attachment. It was important for her to feel vital to her husband, children, and to me, and to feel she cared for us, and dominated and controlled us and would be able to continue to do so. Our relative self-sufficiency threatened her sense of her significance, value, and dominance.

I said, she had come to treatment because of her reaction when her superior had left her. Her analytic work had exposed the feeling that she had sacrificed herself too much in her life, and she had come to feel that her devoted attitude with its associated feeling of being exploited, was unnecessary and unsatisfying. We had also learned that her response to the instances when she had felt helpless during her life had been to take charge, to be in control, so as to become capable of avoiding such painful feelings in the future. Perhaps, I suggested, being a sort of Jane Eyre, a Scheherazade, characters she had particularly admired, toward husband, supervisor, and analyst served to give her a feeling of control. Perhaps my comment meant that she would not be able to continue to assure herself that she could continue to control our relationship and me. Her gratifying illusion about the present and future was threatened by what I had said. Probably her disappointment with the mentor, father, children, husband, and me, came not simply from the lack of gratifying recognition we gave her, but also, from the failure of the situation to support her feeling of being in charge of inferior dependents.

18

Then followed an extended period in which the patient modified her view of the conditions of her life and marriage. She concluded that her husband, decent, loyal, and quite unpsychologically minded, had supported her illusions by seeming to accept her as a guide and mentor, somewhat as her father had done in letting her play at being a sort of surrogate wife when she was merely the older sister and helper with the domestic situation. She found she was relieved more than displeased to note that her children were growing up and out. The analysis would not make it possible for her to realize her childhood and adolescent wishes to be the indispensable member of the family, and to be able to domineer and to control events to avoid disappointment and loss. She grieved, raged, and went through a catalogue of frustrations past and longings for the future. She took more interest and pleasure in her work, her husband, and her garden.

The analysis revealed that passive behavior, which limited her pleasure and gratified her masochistic guilty, and attachment wishes was also meant to conceal and satisfy her childhood wishes to become and remain, the dominating controlling leader of the family and thus live happily ever after. When the possibility of gratifying these wishes came into question in the analysis, anger, resistance, pain, and productive consequences ensued.

A FINAL AND BRIEF EXAMPLE

A successful political figure in his fifties had significant anxiety before writing and delivering speeches, which almost invariably, went well. He received many awards and honors, but he felt there was something hollow about his successes. They never seemed significant to him. He knew he might well feel proud of himself, and satisfied with his achievements, but somehow, he thought he was a pale person in comparison to figures of the past.

He compared himself with Franklin Roosevelt, Maynard Keynes, Enrico Caruso, Marie Curie, and other similar figures, and found himself wanting in comparing his achievements with theirs. In childhood and adolescence he had admired and wished to emulate these people. When asked, as a child prodigy singer, what he wanted to be when he grew up, he thought, "Caruso," and later, someone like Pasteur or Schweitzer and still later, a great political figure.

It became apparent that he had many talents and skills, and a fantasy that he would be able to become anything, even all the things he admired. One of his adult qualities was an enthusiasm for collecting in a wide variety of fields. Another was his tendency to feel a strong sense of nostalgia. At such times he would talk about the great figures of the past, and of past times in a tone of wistful longing. This happened especially after a successful performance he had achieved by dint of great effort, and often, after a happy sexual experience. Why then, did he talk nostalgically and long for a time that never was, for connection with people who never existed in actuality as he thought of them? This question was particularly relevant when one considered that he had been orphaned early, had had multiple homes in childhood, had suffered several painful surgical experiences, and had not really felt happy and safe until his middle years. "Ah," he said, "I'm nostalgic for the time when I believed anything and everything was possible, when I thought, someday I'll make up for it all, for myself, and for everyone else."

DISCUSSION

Little Hans responded to being moved out of the parents' bedroom, to the initial active toddling of his sister, to the loss of his sense of intimacy with his mother, by developing his various horse phobias. His losses and disappointments also included his tonsillectomy, his parents' teasing about his interest in little girls, and castration threats. One aspect of his grappling with his oedipal problem, with the help of his father's Freud-supervised interventions, was expressed in a dream. The Freud-father who interceded in his behalf was a plumber, who would remove his small widdler and bottom, and replace them with larger ones. Hans also said, he would grow up and then he would do everything that grown-ups do with children, like bathe them, or wipe them.

"What do you want to be when you grow up," is a question asked of most children. I answered it when I was Hans' age, by saying, I wanted to be a trolley car conductor. My parents responded by buying me a trolley car conductor outfit, complete with a uniform hat, play tickets, a leather sack, much like those real trolley car conductors carried, and a puncher to punch the tickets. Playing trolley car conductor pleased me. I thought one day I might well actually become one, and when my family rode the trolley cars to visit my grandparents in the nearby town of Perchtoldsdorf, I did not mind that a grownup sold and punched the tickets.

Those Viennese trolley cars are long gone. I never became a trolley conductor, and have to make do with conducting psychoanalyses, a distant though satisfying variant. But I remember the excitement of the trolley cars, and psychoanalysis is no trolley car. Little Hans became a stage director, and I do not doubt that telling people what to do on the stage was, for him, descended from the expressive of, childhood wishes. Probably, Herbert Graf, who had been Little Hans, wanted each production to be better than the last. Maybe he wanted to control, maybe the audience represented his mother who would love and praise him more than she ever had. Maybe some analysands will get better faster because I talk with them about what their wishes and hopeful anticipations are, anticipations that will never come true, as well as about so much else, but none of us will satisfy our preoedipal and oedipal dreams.

Freud revealed something about his variation on the theme. He wrote (1927), "every civilization rests on a compulsion to work and a renunciation of instinct and therefore inevitably provokes opposition . . . rebelliousness and destructive mania" (p. 10). . . . "[External coercion . . . gradually becomes internalized" (p. 11). . . . "[A]rt offers substitutive satisfactions" (p. 14) . . . and serves "to reconcile men . . . to their sacrifices" (p. 10). So wrote the man who had studied Napoleon's campaigns, admired Alexander the Great and Bismarck, followed the fortunes (rather, misfortunes) of the Austrian army, and thought of himself as a Conquistador, the founder of a new science, and leader of an international movement.

He went on (1927), "the most important item in the psychical inventory of a civilization . . . consists . . . in its illusions" (p. 14); "protection against the consequences of his human weakness" (p. 24); "fulfilments of the oldest, strongest and most urgent wishes of mankind . . ." (p. 30). Then he wrote (p. 53), "the primacy of the intellect lies, it is true, in a distant, distant future"; "our science is no illusion" (p. 56). The conquistador had to satisfy himself with hopes about posterity. I leave to you the question, to what extent did the writing of *The Future of an Illusion* have to do with Freud›s illusions and disillusions?

Freud (1925) wrote, "The theory of repression became the cornerstone of our understanding of the neuroses. A different view had now to be taken of the task of therapy. Its aim was no longer to "abreact" an affect which had got on to the wrong lines but to uncover repressions and replace them by acts of judgement which might result either in the accepting or in the condemning of what had formerly been repudiated" (p. 30). Freud's earlier observation, that neurotics were people whose sexual lives were inhibited and unsatisfying, is unchallenged, although the theory that dammed-up libido caused anxiety and symptoms that could be relieved by abreaction has been replaced. But with the appearance of the signal affect theory, and of defense analysis, analytic interest in gratification lessened.

The consequences of frustration, include for instance, learning to put off pleasure till later, to emphasize the potential home run, to take anticipatory pleasure in the anticipated end of the journey, to compensate for the frustration, and make the waiting worthwhile, rather than to attend more to the trip itself. Analytic interest in this attempted resolution as a factor in psychopathology lessened. Fearful unconscious anticipation became more central. Gratifying unconscious fantasies of future pleasures, and the means erected to preserve them, were less studied and emphasized.

The enthusiastic interest in defense is evident in some of the recent psychoanalytic literature (two references under the heading of "gratification" [Mosher, 1991]), and in writings of some of my closest, most admired friends. Thus, we have Brenner (1992), in /a rare hyperbolic moment writing, "in everyday clinical work, one can safely neglect the fact that the concept, ego, embraces more than just defense" (p. 9); and, "when unpleasure arises in association with a drive derivative of childhood origin, a person's mind functions in such a way as to minimize unpleasure while *permitting as much gratification as is compatible with not too much unpleasure*" (p. 15; emphasis added). Conflict and unpleasure minimizing are emphasized and adaptive pleasure seeking is mentioned, acknowledged but not explored to the same degree.

Gray (1992), wrote:

> Freud's (1933) own late revisions of dream theory convey
> a seeming reluctance to bring the definition of the dream
> fully into line with his own revisions of the theory of anxiety
> and intrapsychic conflict. Even today, analysts are tempted
> by tradition to enshrine the brilliant but long-surpassed
> landmark known as "a dream is the *fulfillment* of a wish."
> Freud›s eventual view of the role of anxiety in the solution of
> intrapsychic conflict leads us inexorably to a new definition
> of the dream: *A dream is the ego's response that thwarts the id's
> attempt to gratify a conflicted wish* [p. 325].

Gray's view that technique should be centered on exploration of
distress, not on interpreting the nature of concealed gratification
seems overstated in this instance.

Cooper (1992) wrote, "[paranoia is] an available defensive mode
that can appear in varying degrees of intensity, whenever there is a
threat to higher-level narcissistic defenses" (p. 438). And, "The need
of patients at some point in the analysis to feel that the analyst is
malignantly withholding, or torturing, or controlling, represents
attempts to experience themselves as powerful enough to be yielding
only to an object of such grand dimensions, to assure themselves that
the world is exactly as predicted, and to protect a fragile self from the
hazards of intimacy (p. 441)." These citations taken from authors of
differing theoretical preferences show that anxiety due to anticipation
of danger, and defense, is often the center of analytic interest, and that
pleasure seeking is relatively neglected.

The view that gratification is essential, and that illusion is a part
of it, remained integral to child analysis, with its games, presents, and

a more interactive analyst long after abreaction was abandoned as the therapeutic goal. Winnicott (1960) wrote:

> The good-enough mother meets the omnipotence of the infant and to some extent makes sense of it... The mother who is not good enough is not able to implement the infant's omnipotence, and so she repeatedly fails to meet the infant gesture; instead she substitutes her own gesture which is to be given sense by the compliance of the infant [p. 145]....
>
> *In the first case the mother's adaptation is good enough* and in consequence the infant begins to believe in external reality which appears and behaves as by magic (because of the mother›s relatively successful adaptation to the infant›s gestures and needs), and which acts in a way that does not clash with the infant›s omnipotence. On this basis, the infant can abrogate omnipotence... The infant can now begin to enjoy the *illusion* of omnipotent creating and controlling, and then can gradually come to recognize the illusory element, the fact of playing and imagining [p. 146].

Winnicott wrote of infancy, not adult analyses, and his "imagining" did not explicitly state that imagining and anticipating the desired outcome is pleasurable, that it contributes substantially to the maintenance of psychological comfort, is protected, and rests on maintaining illusion. Thereby, he left me the opportunity to be Winnicottian and do so.

In a recent presentation, Blum (1994) noted, "Daydreams usually afford a high yield of pleasure, comparable to the 'castles in the air' of the child, and daydreams may be regarded as intimate, cherished possessions... the daydream, or conscious fantasy [creates]... a future situation which represents a wish-fulfillment. . . ." I add, the unconscious anticipation of the expected future is gratifying. Daydreams, play, and unconscious fantasy are gratifying among other reasons, because, they anticipate future pleasure. If the subject thought the anticipated pleasure would never be actualized, the dreams, daydreams, unconscious fantasies would be far less gratifying.

CONCLUSION

Though psychoanalysts generally subscribe to the idea that mental functioning seeks to maximize pleasure and minimize unpleasure, active, purposeful pleasure seeking seems to receive less attention in writings on technique than does unpleasure avoidance motivated by anxious anticipations of danger, guilt, and other forms of suffering.

Conscious and unconscious anticipations of pleasure to come are pleasurable. To the extent that such anticipations include imagining and anticipating the gratification of childhood wishes, they depend on hope and illusion. Resistance to modifying such illusion-laden anticipations, deserves more attention and interpretation. Fear of loss of illusions could well be added to the fears of loss due to object loss, loss of the object's love, castration, and superego condemnation.

Analytic interventions can confront the patient with the unpleasant truth that counting on expected pleasures that will never come is unrealistic. The process of disillusionment such interventions trigger can be painful. Like other threatening anticipations of loss, the anticipation of the loss of satisfaction contingent on loss of illusions of future ratification can trigger anger, fear, and resistance. Disillusionment can also result in changes in viewpoints, theories, and attitudes so that these come to correspond better to practical possibilities. Analysts favor such changes, and in order to help the patient to revise himself, we should accept the inevitability of resistance to disillusionment, as well as its necessary and beneficial aspects.

REFERENCES

Blum, H. (1994). The clinical value of daydreams and their role in character analysis. Paper presented at the New York University Psychoanalytic Society, September.

Brenner, C. (1992). The mind as conflict and compromise formation. Paper presented at the New York Psychoanalytic Society, December 8.

Burns, R. (1786). To a louse on seeing one in a lady's bonnet. *Complete Poems of Robert Burns*. New York: Crowell, 1884, p. 74.

Cooper, A. (1992), Paranoia: A part of most analyses *Journal of the American Psychoanalytic Association* 41:423–442.

Freud, S. (1916). Some character-types met with in psycho-analytic work. *Standard Edition*, 14:309–333. London: Hogarth Press, 1957.

——— (1917). Fixation to traumas—the unconscious. *Standard Edition*, 16:273–285. London: Hogarth Press, 1959.

——— (1925). An Autobiographical Study. *Standard Edition*, 20:1–71. London: Hogarth Press, 1959.

——— (1927). The Future of an Illusion. *Standard Edition*, 21:1–56. London: Hogarth Press, 1959.

——— (1933). Revision of the theory of dreams. *Standard Edition*, 22:7–30, London: Hogarth Press, 1964.

Gray, P. (1992). Memory as a resistance and the telling of a dream. *Journal of the American Psychoanalytic Association* 40:307–327.

Mosher, P., Ed. (1991). *Title, Key Word and Author Index to Psychoanalytic Journals 1920-90.* New York: American Psychoanalytic Association.

Reiser, M. (1986). The durable core of Freud's empirical science. 38th Brill Memorial Lecture, presented at the New York Psychoanalytic Society, November 11.

Rothstein, A. (1991). On some relationships of fantasies of perfection to the calamities of childhood. *Int. J. Psycho-Anal.*, 72:313–323.

Tarachow, S. (1962). Interpretation and reality in psychotherapy. *Int. J. Psycho-Anal.*, 62:377–387.

Winnicott, D. (1960), Ego distortion in terms of true and false self. In: *The Maturational Processes and the Facilitating Environment.* New York: International Universities Press, pp. 140–152.

CHAPTER 2

The Influence of Parents' Unconscious Fantasies on Children's Adaptation as Illustrated by Transsexuality

(1992). *Journal of Clinical Psychoanalysis*, 1(4):547–559
The Influence of Parents' Unconscious Fantasies on
Children's Adaptation as Illustrated by Transsexuality

In his paper, "The Unconscious," in 1915, Freud wrote "It is a very remarkable thing that the Ucs. of one human being can react on that of another, without passing through the Cs. This deserves closer investigation" (p. 194).

Freud's observation was probably influenced by his experience as a hypnotist. Freud was impressed that suggestions can affect hypnotic subjects. The hypnotist can evoke memories, unavailable in the subject's waking state, and he can suggest behavior to be performed by the subject after the trance is lifted. In the posthypnotic state, what was recalled under hypnosis disappears, as does awareness of the hypnotic suggestions. Responses to the hypnotic suggestions appear, and the waking persons invent explanations to account for their post-hypnotic actions.

Similar phenomena occur in daily life. Humorists Elaine May and Mike Nichols depicted guilt-inducing parents who consciously had only affectionate desires, but whose covert messages influenced their children, themselves consciously oblivious to the hidden messages transmitted by the parents' behavior. The guilt-inducing mother who needs no-one to change the light bulb because, she says, she is glad to sit in the dark, is, by now, an obvious example of the power of covert intentions.

Recent psychoanalytic developments, as in the contributions of Kris (1956), Hartmann (1964), Stein (1981), Brenner (1982), and McDevitt (1985), to give only a few examples, have emphasized that unconscious fantasies are expressed covertly in character traits, in interests and preferences, in persistent behavior, as well as in transitory disturbing phenomena, like slips, symptoms, and mood alterations. Arlow (1979) has made especially suggestive comments about how patients evoke responses in their analysts, where both the evoking factors and the responses reflect the power of unconscious forces.

Many recent studies emphasize the important influence of object relations in development, and the benefit of assessing the influence of the analyst's unconscious motivations on patient—analyst interrelationships, and hence on the course of analyses. The results of such investigations press us to the following conclusion. Genetic and dynamic understanding of patients requires recognition of the important interactions between subtle, unrecognized behavioral reflections of patients' unconscious fantasy organizations, and those of important people in their past and present lives, the analyst included.

Analysts of adults have opportunities to show patients how their unconscious motives enter into their fantasies and how their fantasies influence their behavior, particularly in the transference, and to a lesser degree, in their daily lives. Withholding, passive aggression, provocation, and other unconsciously motivated behaviors of patients evoke wished-for responses from others who are often quite unaware of what made them angry, aroused, or guilty.

Sometimes I have had the opportunity to learn how patients' unconscious fantasies influence their parenting. Parents are often motivated to learn more about themselves because they wish to understand more about their conflicted relations with their children. As an example, a mother was interested to learn that her child's fear of separating was fostered by herself because she unconsciously wished the child to remain a docile companion. In another instance, a father learned that he unconsciously encouraged a child to act out his own conflicted antisocial desires.

Similarly, working with many patients has convinced me that it is often important to construct and discuss what covert motivations their parents and other important figures have expressed, and what effects these parental adaptations had on the patients during their development. Others, like Tyson (1977) and Poland (1992), have noted such instances.

Hypotheses about unconscious motivations in people who are not present, but were or are important to the patients, are harder to support than are hypotheses about unconscious motivations in the patients themselves, since these can be manifest in transferences and evoked countertransference attitudes. When the important objects are alive, however, and continue to interact with the analytic patient, at least some supportive or contradicting data can appear as the patient tests his theories about these people in direct contact with them.

Child analysts have been interested in the interrelationships between parents' unconscious fantasies and those of their children. Sometimes, when parents and children have been in analysis concurrently, discussions among analysts and supervisors about the case have been possible. In several such cases, the powerful and specific effects of parents' unconscious fantasies upon their children's adaptations—as reflected in interests, sexual attitudes, and symptomatology has been demonstrated convincingly.

It is impossible here to describe several concurrent analyses in detail. The recognizability of the people involved is increased in such situations, and the possibilities for disguising without excessive falsification of data is diminished. I find it very difficult to present case reports of analyses I have conducted. It is hard to present material sufficiently specific and detailed to persuade an audience of conclusions even in a single analysis.

Therefore, I intend to use an autobiographical account written by Renée Richards to illustrate conclusions I have reached in work with patients, as well as through private case discussions, reports from concurrent analyses of parents and children, published material, and information from my own analysis. During her personal analyses, Richards had the opportunity to observe her parents in action, and to test some speculations about them. Richards' parents were not subtle. Therefore, we outside observers may derive similar impressions about some, in this case, not so hidden meanings of Richards' parents' manifest behavior.

I will try to show how parental influences on the child Richards covertly expressed certain of the parents' unconscious wishes and conflicts, that is, their unconscious fantasies, and tended to encourage some tendencies and discourage others in Richards. I propose that Richards' mother sought to counteract fears of dependency and vulnerability and to derive gratification of competitive and sensual wishes through establishing support in reality for the unconscious idea that she was independent and powerful, because she was male as well as female. She dressed and acted as both woman and man, behaved seductively, dominated and controlled, and the acceptance of her behavior by those around her, especially her children, provided the confirmation in reality that her unconscious solution required.

Richards' father, I suggest, enacted the part of a sexless person, who, through his submissive behavior, countered and paid for his aggressive inclinations, even though these occasionally erupted.

Richards constructed his adaptation in relation to this context. He exhibited clinging behavior in early childhood, later attempted to ingratiate himself by imitating his parents, and later still, added satisfactions of guilty needs for punishment, assertions of independence and power, and provocative aggressiveness to manifestly consistent sexual and gender behavior.

Renée Richards published *Second Serve,* an autobiography, in 1983 when she was 39, to shed light on the development of her transsexual adaptation. It includes a great deal of personal history, informed by understandings derived from two analyses.

Richards tells us her mother had wanted a son. Five years before Richards' birth, she had borne a daughter who was given a boy's name. Though she wanted a son, "All her life she had been in conflict with the world of men" (p. 1). Her labor with Richards began with a massive hemorrhage. She drove herself a good distance to the hospital, where placenta praevia was diagnosed. The obstetrician recommended maceration and removal of the child because a Caesarean was considered excessively dangerous. Richards' mother insisted on the Caesarean, which was, incidentally, performed by a woman, without the participation of men. Richards wrote that his mother "risked death twice" to bear her son, and that thereby, she showed such "courage" that, "Perhaps I've been running to catch up ever since" (p. 5).

Richards notes, "If I sat down to write a case history of an imaginary transsexual, I could not come up with a more provocative set of circumstances than that of my childhood" (p. 5). If transsexualism is someday proven to be biochemical, "I will . . . conclude that fate has a sense of humor because my early life is strewn with unsubtle touches that beg to be seen as reasons for my sexual confusion. If they aren't the true cause, they ought to be" (p. 5).

The household consisted of Richards' mother, sister, aunt, grandmother, a maid and a nurse, all women, and a father who largely absented himself. Richards writes that his father was a compliant husband who wanted to escape "the smothering control of his wife who utterly dominated the household and with whom he never won an argument." Another evidence of the father's submissiveness was that Richards' father claimed he had sacrificed a potential academic career he desired for himself to earn money to support his wife's residency training as a psychiatrist. The young Richards thought his father weak, and that he could not look to him for help. The young boy felt he was "on my own." Richards felt isolated and inadequate, feelings he continued to experience often during later life.

Both parents worked as physicians all day. Richards early understood that his parents were often unavailable, and he became very sensitive to separations. In the mornings, the small, lonely child would crawl into the parents' bed. When mother awoke "in a languorous way," young Richards could watch her wash, dress her hair, scent and powder her body, put on her underthings, and then proceed to put on her "shell," no lipstick, a severe blouse, a suit with padded shoulders and flat heavy shoes.

At dinner, mother retransformed herself, now wearing low-cut evening dresses that showed off her bosom. Many aspects of Richards' dress, eating, and bowel habits were controlled by the mother. She apparently wished to be admired from a distance as a female, obeyed as a superior, and recognized as at least as powerful as any man. Her seductive and domineering behavior, and the distance she maintained were constant aspects of the context in which the children had to adapt.

Meanwhile, his sister was dressed like a boy and encouraged to be a tomboy except on social occasions, when, to her distress, she had to wear feminine clothes. The mother encouraged both children to develop a sense of being of both sexes, similar to the role she enacted herself, though she accepted Richards' expression of maleness less than that of femaleness.

The sister mounted surprise attacks on Richards, giving him blows to the head, roughhoused with him in an exciting and frightening game in which she pinned him down and smothered him with a pillow "brutalizing and nearly killing me." She teasingly dressed him in her clothes, including underwear, often in the mother's presence. The behavior seems to have been encouraged by the mother, and to have been overtly sexual, with the sister playing the part of a male. The sister also repeatedly played a game of pushing his penis inside his body and saying, "See, you're not a little boy, you're a little girl" (pp. 12–13). The frightened and seduced boy, loving, influenced by fear and wishing to be loved, soon accepted that the female was powerful and attractive. The compliant love relation with his sister and mother became a model for later social and sexual relationships.

> My father was so big and gruff and strong, yet so prone to crumble under pressure. My mother was so soft and yielding in her womanly guise, so cold and intellectual as a professional, yet so ready to enter into a screaming argument at home. My sister was so obviously a girl, yet trying so hard to be a boy. The rest of the family members were simply overpowered by this insanity. They moved about the house as if it were perfectly normal, and I looked on wondering why I couldn't adjust [p. 13].

The family accepted fantasy as reality.

I suggest that Richards' mother unconsciously regarded herself as both male and female. She dressed both parts, and acted as though having children and raising them were her exclusive province in which her husband had no significant part. She encouraged both her children to adopt the same aims. They were to be male, female, and totally self-sufficient, though at the same time controlled and dominated by her.

The father, meanwhile, gruff, critical, and angry in a seemingly masculine way, was also passive, compliant, unsatisfied, demanding, and guilt provoking. Among his unconscious fantasy solutions, I propose, was that he was unsexual and unaggressive, powerless, benevolent, suffering and harmless. His aggressive competitive attitude with Richards was sometimes expressed directly, and generally covertly, as he gave his son to his wife as an offering, to be dominated.

At age 4, Richards guiltily enjoyed being dressed as a girl by his sister. The joy came partly because of the affection he received at such times and through the sexual excitement he experienced in the game, similar to that which he had experienced in watching his mother dress. His acceptance of the role also allowed him to avert his

sister's attacks. He was also terrified of revealing his pleasure, because open sexual or self-assertive gratification was prohibited.

His mother forced him to wear girls' clothing as a Hallowe'en party costume, to his great humiliation. Mother also administered weekly enemas. At the same time, physical courage, athletic prowess, and perfect academic achievement, which he rarely attained, were demanded. He wanted to be courageous, like his mother. He was repeatedly subjected to criticism and isolation for supposed shortcomings. Overall, his parents gave him more support than criticism as far as academic and athletic ability were concerned, a condition that encouraged his outstanding, if conflicted, accomplishments in those areas. They demanded submission, not enterprise in other areas.

At age 6, aggression and guilt entered the picture. Richards now began to do himself, what his sister had done with him before. He secretly dressed himself in his sister's clothes. This activity was accompanied by fearful thoughts of being sneaky and rebellious. Cross-dressing was permissible only if pleasure was concealed, and if it was done in the sister's presence, at her behest. Thus cross-dressing now represented self-assertion and rebellion, and compliance at the same time.

By age 10, Richards noted another change. Screaming fights with mother began to occur. "My mother took to giving me an occasional cuff on the head." Once, "I ran away and stayed with friends for a few days" (p. 26). The cross-dressing and the flight response both helped him feel that he could exist independently, and, ostensibly, demonstrated that his solitude was his choice, not a misery imposed on him. Richards' self-consoling, hostile rebellion that took the form of cross-dressing, running away, and isolating himself resembled the isolation the parents had earlier imposed by physical absence and inability to make much emotional contact. It apparently served as an ingratiation, a joining with both parents in shared fantasies, as well as a provocation, a going beyond their wishes, and was a manifestation of courage. It could only come when maturing capacities made it possible.

It also represented a variety of masculine identification. Like his harmless father, he never won an argument with his mother. Being isolated imposed a cost. It limited his investment and pleasure in other people. It implied attachment and loyalty to his parents, and imposed difficulty in constructing more gratifying social relationships.

Richards often resorted to cross-dressing when he expected to be, or had been, criticized for some shortcoming, as in athletic performance. He took such criticisms to mean that failures and also independent successes were disapproved. The shortcomings and not the accomplishments drew attention. There was no masturbation or overtly sexual fantasy. However, during his latency period a conscious fantasy, derived from a story mother told him, seemed to provide a channel for his adaptation.

"A little girl who performed on a trapeze was injured, and her place had to be taken by a boy. He selflessly donned the girl's costume and performed her act... I used to imagine that I was that little boy, thrust by forces beyond my control into the role of a little girl, but with the approval of my family" (p. 28).

Any hint of aggressive wishes to injure the girl, or of the exhibitionistic sexual excitement of the trapeze artist, the element of exhibitionistic competition with the mother, and the angry submission were all concealed behind the defensive use of idealistic, virtuous selflessness. The fantasy solution complied with parental preferences and assured Richards of approval, while, at the same time, it enabled him unconsciously to satisfy sexual and aggressive wishes.

In prepuberty, Richards "still didn't feel completely real" (p. 30) when observing himself in a mirror, dressed as a girl. His attempt to harmonize his inner conflicts resulted in the idea that he had two personae, Dick and Renée. During lonely afternoons, when no one was in the house, he dressed as a girl and went out to interact with transients—"shopkeepers, clerks and other pedestrians... Renée fed on them because they represented a casual and ready acceptance of her femaleness" (p. 31). His feminine appearance was accepted as fact by others. This acceptance, though only a limited substitute for parental love, was extremely important to him. He enacted the role of the girl on the trapeze. Again he actively did what he had passively suffered earlier, when he had been forcibly dressed as a girl and exposed at the Hallowe'en party.

He was once discovered by his aunt and once by his sister. They displayed little response. "The increasing risks I took were probably an unconscious bid for recognition—for some support—but it was not forthcoming" (p. 32). Richards' unconscious appeals did not produce the loving concern he wanted to arouse in his family or even the angry response he feared, and perhaps also hoped, to provoke. He remained isolated. The failure of cross-dressing to gain the kind of critical response some of his accomplishments evoked must have reinforced his belief that cross-dressing was desired. At the same time, the communal acceptance of his masquerade gratified and validated his internal fantasy. In fantasy, he was boy and girl, like his mother, and harmless, like his father. Like his parents, he sought social confirmation to affirm his unconscious attempts to harmonize conflicting wishes.

"Once, when I was fifteen I overheard my sister ask my mother, 'What do you do with men who want to be a woman?' My mother answered, 'You send them to Scandinavia'" (p. 33). As with the trapeze fantasy, he later took up this idea as a suggestion by his mother, suitably adaptable to his ongoing need to defy submissively and to deal with incompatible unconscious wishes by creating appearances that could be validated socially.

Puberty occurred at 16. An orgasm in mutual masturbation with a girl schoolmate was his first ejaculation while awake, and was a "great leap in the right direction" (p. 38). But the girl blamed him and would not see him again and "This . . . badly undercut my confidence. Renée took advantage and stepped up her schedule of appearances" (p. 39). What another person might have taken as partial success, Richards reacted to as to an infraction. Rebellious and delinquent experiences were limited to being with friends while they performed hostile actions, but even vicarious participation enhanced his sense of his dangerous capacity to do harm, which he counterbalanced by adopting more overtly receptive and childlike masochistic behavior.

When Richards' sister went away to college, he became buddies with a male schoolmate, with whom he slept in his sister's bed, where the two also roughhoused in a way similar to his early play with the sister. "Barry would invariably recapture and subdue me . . . so that he could hold me absolutely immobile" (p. 45). The parents restricted themselves to coming into the room and "solemnly" asking for "a little more quiet." "There was never any obvious sexual excitement," a tribute to Richards' capacity to suppress awareness of his sexual feelings (p. 45). The wish to be with his feared and loved sister, and to negate his gratification at her being gone, I hypothesize, contributed to this behavior. Much later, he could, as a woman, openly gratify the once unconscious sexual desires of this game in sexual intercourse.

Meanwhile, at 15, he was frightened when reading Krafft-Ebbing, who described people with Richards' condition as lunatics. This seemed to him to support his idea that his sexuality made him a dangerous criminal, bound to be despised by the community. At 17, the rediscovery of the possibility of a surgical transformation gave him a hope of resolving his conflicting wishes, by putting an end to his "Dick" aspect.

He countered pubertal changes by heavy adhesive tape and string, which he used to pull his penis back out of sight, with sufficient force to create a groove he thought resembled the female external genital appearance, and to cause painful "bruises, hemorrhages and abrasions" (p. 57). Richards continued to suffer from both parents' criticism and rejection. "Once at age seventeen when I had lost a tennis match, father's tactless comments included the phrase, 'I am ashamed of you.' Even his offhand remarks could sometimes be devastating, as when he once commented, 'Your back is just like your mother's'" (p. 58).

At this point, in my view, the transsexual practices, of which an important component was looking at himself in a mirror, seemed to serve a variety of functions. Among these were self-soothing by means of replicating affectionate times, as when he watched his mother dress, and played with his sister. The practices also gratified hostile wishes to rebel and compete, reflected in the idea that he would shock and horrify if he revealed his behavior. Because he could act without his family's knowledge, and exclude them as he felt excluded, he could simultaneously enact hostile and self-soothing wishes and submissive requirements. His transsexual behavior also supported the idea that appearance, when supported by the belief of others in it, defines reality. His conscious wish was to take the role of the female copulating with a male.

What he did, I hypothesize, represented self-punishment, directly, through his physical self-abuse, and through fantasy, in that he accepted the Krafft-Ebbing judgment that he was a lunatic, adding his own idea that he was a criminal. This satisfied a need for punishment, motivated by guilt, apparently over unconscious competitive anger at his attacking, depreciating father, mother, and sister, at being controlled and dominated, and over his incompletely suppressed sexual desires. His behavior also gratified sexual wishes to be acted upon sexually as his mother and sister had acted on him. It also supported his suppression of his actual, threatening, sexual feelings in that he insisted that his gender, not his sexuality and aggressivity, was the main problem issue. It gave him the feeling of being in control and self-sufficient, not subject to others' whims or to disappointments. It made his isolation bearable, because it was self-imposed, made him unique, and satisfied his parents. It supported him in his ideal of being courageous by bearing pain.

During Richards' medical internship, his mother was diagnosed as having an inoperable cancer. At the end of the internship year, Richards entered analysis with Robert Bak. "As our relationship was established, Dr. Bak outlined his theory about the cause of my sexual confusion. I was afraid of losing my penis. My transformation into a woman was a way of acting out that fear... what I liked about the process was not becoming a woman but the relief I felt when I changed back to a man..." (p. 121). "Dr. Bak's presentation was so convincing that I accepted his interpretation... but this did not help me... my desire to be a woman increased" (p. 122).

In fact, Richards was not convinced. He wanted to be a man as Bak said, but he wanted to be a woman too. He wrote, in obvious mockery, that Bak's explanation reminded him of the story of the man who banged his head against the wall because stopping felt so good.

Meanwhile, his mother became sicker. Richards spent much time with her, and he felt he had achieved some understanding and forgiveness of her. "I brought this up with Dr. Bak, but he had no comment" (p. 129). Richards seems to imply that Bak's understanding of him was too simple. It failed to take account of the helpful, idealistic, and affectionate wishes that Richards expressed in caring for his mother, and in specific choices in work (after all, both parents were doctors), play, and relationships as well as in sexuality. Among other things, he wanted to be a good child, and a constructive person.

During Richards' first residency year, his mother died, and "After mother's death, Renée became even harder to control" (p. 130). The death of Richards' mother affected him as, earlier, his sister's departure for college had, and as later, Bak's death would. The analysis did not help with this. In a reprise of his presenting himself as female and childlike, as he had done when his sister went off to college, Richards cross-dressed more flamboyantly, had suicidal thoughts, and eventually, apparently two years or so after his mother's death, terminated his analysis and contacted the surgeon who had transformed Christine Jorgensen.

However, for years afterwards, Richards alternately presented the physical attributes of both sexes, sometimes using hormones to become more womanlike, sometimes eliminating them to become more manlike. He had sexual relations with women, found homosexual experiences unsatisfying, and after repeatedly failing to find a surgeon who would perform the transsexual transformation, he married, had breast reduction surgery, and fathered a son. He phoned Bak to inform him he had become a father. Bak wished him well.

Bak died in October 1974. In the following spring, Richards succeeded in becoming surgically transformed, and with much struggle, persuaded much of the community to accept him as what he claimed he now was, a woman. He could play tennis as a woman, and play the woman's part in sexual intercourse with a man, and yet, he was also a father. In this way, he had achieved his mother's fantasy of being both sexes, and his father's fantasy that he was acted upon. Richards' transformation also enabled him to participate in a social movement. He fought discrimination based on sexual preference, displaying the courage he had admired in his mother, satisfying moral ideals, and feeling a part of a community.

The following are the main points I have tried to make. Unconscious fantasy solutions of psychic conflicts influence behavior. Parents, consciously unaware of purposeful covert aspects of their behavior, influence the adaptation of their children. They encourage some attitudes and behaviors in their children, and discourage others, without being aware of what they are doing. Sexual attitudes and behaviors are among those which children form in the context of their relations with their parents and other important people in the course of development. The children are unaware, consciously, of what they are adapting to, and they are unaware, as well, of much of the purpose of their manifest behavior, including its covert aspects.

I have used Renée Richards' autobiography as an example of a general situation, because undisguised, detailed analytic supporting data cannot be revealed.

References

Arlow, J. A. (1979). The genesis of interpretation. *Journal of the American Psychoanalytic Association* 27(Suppl.): 195–207.

Brenner, C. (1982). *The Mind in Conflict*. New York: International Universities Press.

Freud, S. (1915). The unconscious. *Standard Edition*, 14:159–216. London: Hogarth Press, 1957.

Hartmann, H. (1964). *Essays on Ego Psychology*. New York: International Universities Press.

Kris, E. (1956). The recovery of childhood memories. *Psychoanalytic Study of the Child* 11:54–89. New York: International Universities Press.

McDevitt, J. D. (1985). Pre–oedipal determinants of an infantile gender disorder. Paper presented at the International Symposium on Separation-Individuation, Paris, France, November 3, 1985.

Poland, W. S. (1992). Transference: "An original creation." *Psychoanal. Q.*, 61:185–206.

Richards, R. (1983). *Second Serve*. New York: Stein & Day.

Stein, M. H. (1981). The unobjectionable part of the transference. *Journal of the American Psychoanalytic Association* 29:869–892.

Tyson, P. L. (1977). Notes on the analysis of a prelatency boy with a dog phobia. *Psychoanalytic Study of the Child* 32:427–458.

CHAPTER 3

Technical Considerations in Treating Patients with Character Disorders

Kafka, E. (1991). Chapter 5: Technical Considerations in Treating Patients with Character Disorders. Conflict and Compromise: Therapeutic Implications. In *Conflict and Compromise: Therapeutic Implications*, edited by Scott Dowling. Madison Connecticut: International Universities Press, pp 65–76.

Nonpsychotic, nonorganic psychopathologies have generally been subdivided into symptomatic disorders and character disorders. In symptomatic disorders, the subject makes a self-diagnosis of psychopathology, often based on an estimation that painful affects such as anxiety, guilt, shame, or depressive feelings of low self-esteem are excessive, given the conditions under which they arise, and/or that they cause inhibitions of action. For instance, a person may conclude that the level of anxiety he experiences in anticipating an examination or an airplane trip is more severe than he can explain as proportional to the risk he judges to be associated with the activity that is feared, and that this contributes to a restriction of performance. Such patients wish to be relieved of specific complaints and are consciously motivated to seek help.

In character disorders, certain activities may feel impulsive to the subject. Other activities may fail to produce the conditions they are consciously intended to achieve, or may have unwelcome consequences. Sometimes people with such character structure seek therapy because they conclude they are failing to live up to their capacities, as when careers or social relationships do not advance satisfactorily. Sometimes they are induced to seek. help by relatives, friends, teachers, or others, who persuade them that their behavior is getting them into trouble of one kind of another, or that they are not managing to live up to their potential for gratification or success.

Failed romantic attachments, difficulties in adapting to changing circumstances, or repeated, seemingly inexplicable unwanted responses on the part of offspring or authorities may induce such a person to seek consultation. Alternatively, this type of individual may need the advice of others in spite of having little or no understanding that he may be provoking the unwelcome social consequences and/or may be rejecting those he consciously wishes to attract. Often enough, such patients have no specific complaints, are uncertain that anything is wrong with them, or feel pushed into treatment by others. Given their uncertain motivation, introducing such patients to treatment often involves difficulties. The recommendation that the therapist should strive to make their ego syntonic but problematic behavior more ego alien is often difficult to follow.

The therapist knows that the two categories of patients—those with symptom disorders and those with character disorders—are not as dissimilar as they may seem on the surface. The therapist will understand that unconscious conflicts affect all manifestations of behavior, including thoughts and associated feelings and acts, and not only symptomatic expressions. He or she may well anticipate that the symptomatic patient who accepts treatment will soon discover he or she also has character problems, and that the patient who presents with character problems will soon discover symptomatic restrictions or avoidances.

In both types of presenting complaint, the therapist has the advantage of knowing that the symptoms and the behaviors the patient employs are manifestations of unconscious conflicts that might be more successfully resolved if they could be revealed to the patient and better understood. The task is to discover and help the patient understand her or his unconscious conflicts and their unwanted, as well as useful, effects. It behooves the therapist to be attuned to signs of unconscious conflict.

Signs of unconscious conflict are many, though often subtle. They include slips of the tongue, dreams, embarrassments, hesitations and suppressions in talking of certain matters, pressured speech or impulsive acts, signs of the irrational in symptoms, seemingly inexplicable painful affects, transference prejudgments, and other evidences. Demonstrating such signs to the patient may lead the patient to the understanding of how unconscious wishes, fears, and defenses enter into unconscious conflicts and affect everyday behavior.

In people with character disorders, symptomatic evidences are absent or subtle and may be difficult to demonstrate. However, one phenomenon on the border between symptomatic and seemingly reasonable behavior, which is to say, transference distortion, is ubiquitous. Every patient has a variant of the symptomatic in the transference attitude. This may involve, among other possible attitudes, fear, unusual admiration, curiosity, or embarrassment. The patient may regard the therapist as having no emotional life.

Patients' theories and feelings are reflected in their behaviors toward treatment and the therapist, and reveal irrational prejudgments. Often enough, patients can see that their attitudes are irrational. They can accept that the treatment situation is not actually as frightening as they think, or as potentially gratifying as they wish, and this realization can help them accept the fact that they are profoundly influenced by unconscious factors. If parallels between transferences and behaviors in ordinary life can be demonstrated to exist, patients with character disorders are likely to become more motivated to understand their unconscious mentation, and to accept the labor and discomfort this pursuit occasions. Careful attention to and tactful interpretation of transference distortions can go a long way toward helping patients with character disorders become more aware of their fears and avoidances, and helps them recognize the unconscious, often undesirable gratifications their behavior affords them.

Two clinical illustrations follow. In both cases, the material is disguised to preserve confidentiality, and selected and abstracted for the sake of focusing on the point to be illustrated, that is to say, that careful demonstration of the paradoxical and prejudgmental elements revealed through transference manifestations is a particularly valuable tool in the treatment of patients with character problems, whose conscious motivation for treatment is not great.

CLINICAL ILLUSTRATION 1

The patient was a professional woman in her early forties. She had been involved for eight years in a relationship with a man ten years her junior. This had begun shortly after her divorce from her husband, whom she married at age twenty-four while in graduate school. The marriage had been amicable but not passionate, although the sexual aspects were described as satisfying. The patient believed she was eager to have a family. However, the husband steadfastly refused to have children. He claimed that his experience as a child of divorced parents had convinced him that having a family would be undesirable for him, and he preferred to devote his energy to his professional life, which required a great deal of travel, and which he found sufficiently gratifying. At thirty-five, the patient reached the decision that her wish to have a family and a closer relationship with a man meant that she would have to look elsewhere, and the couple divorced as a consequence of that conclusion.

The patient soon became involved with her current companion, who was a junior in her office when they met, and who had, in the intervening time, achieved approximately her own level of responsibility. This man had been importuning her to marry him for several years, but the patient seemed unable to make up her mind. She wondered whether he might be too young, or whether she loved him as much as he loved her, or whether having a child with him might be a mistake. She had discussed her inability to make up her mind with the man, and with various friends, and they had persuaded her to try professional help. However, she was unconvinced that anything was wrong with her.

After explaining her situation in the early interviews, the patient went on to complain that one reason why she thought treatment would be unlikely to help, beyond the fact that there was really nothing wrong with her, was that she thought that the conditions of treatment were unfair and degrading. She objected to the idea that she would have to pay for missed sessions even if her absence were to be caused by illnesses or work responsibilities. She could not understand why the therapist had the right to select the time for his vacation, while, if she took time off, she would both miss her appointments and have to pay for them. She objected to the notion that the appointment schedule could not be easily altered.

I responded that, certainly, embarking on treatment meant that she would have to make certain concessions, but that the advantages might be worth the trouble. As to fees, missed appointments would have to be paid for only if the hours could not be filled, and I would try to be as flexible as possible about making up hours or changing them if she could provide reasonable advance notice. Somewhat mollified, the patient agreed to try, and a three-times-a-week schedule began.

The patient then proceeded to describe the history of her development. She was the older of two children, having a brother five years younger. Her parents were both in their mid-thirties when they married. Her mother, a nurse, gave up work when she became pregnant shortly after her marriage, but often complained about having no career. Both parents were eager to have children and they were delighted when the patient was born, though it turned out that both would have preferred a boy. In the event, repeated attempts at another pregnancy soon followed, but, when the patient reached puberty, and discussions about sexuality and pregnancy came to take place, she learned that conception had been difficult for her mother, and that several miscarriages had occurred before a brother was conceived, and born.

The patient claimed to have no memory of her mother's pregnancy, or of the birth of the eagerly desired son, but a later story was that she was disappointed that the baby was a boy, rather than a girl who would be a better playmate. Her memory of her relationship with her brother in childhood revolved mainly around instances when she felt she had to make concessions to him, such as baby-sitting in her early teens, when she would have preferred more freedom, or tutoring him in school subjects, or having to attend his performances as a Little League ballplayer.

I asked whether her feeling of being put-upon and having to make concessions in relation to therapy resembled her feelings about having had to be too accommodating in relation to her brother.

The patient responded that she felt burdened then and now when she was unfairly restricted, but that any other similarity was coincidental. She went on to describe her current romantic relationship as involving similar restrictions about which she also felt resentful. Her companion had been more cooperative in the past, but since he had been awarded a series of promotions, he had demanded more and more concessions from her on the ground that he had to work late and travel for business; therefore, he often could not take an equal share of the domestic duties. I commented that her lover, like her brother and me, seemed to her to demand excessive concessions. She agreed, and added that her evaluations at work generally reflected still another arena in which excessive demands were made on her. She was usually congratulated on her effectiveness but she was also informed that her unwillingness to take on responsibility, which she usually thought of as an unwillingness to be exploited, stood in the way of her advancement.

She responded to my remark that the work situation was evidently yet another setting in which she thought excessive demands were made, by telling me that my comment only proved her point, inasmuch as I evidently thought her unreasonable, and wanted to add my critical voice to those of others. She added that now, having experienced two months of treatment with no benefit, she was planning to stop coming, especially since a vacation she had planned before starting with me was coming up, and she had no intention of paying for the time.

I expressed surprise that she had not mentioned this plan before. The patient said she thought there would have been no point in doing so. She had had to pay for her trip in advance, and couldn't change her time off from her job because the whole thing had been arranged months before. I pointed out that she seemed to be making an assumption about my attitude. Did she believe I would demand that she revise an unrevisable arrangement she had made before starting treatment? Indeed she did, she said. If she had been mistaken, she would continue the treatment.

Other examples of mistaken prejudgments appeared. In one instance, the patient alluded to having received a promotion months after the event, and when I expressed surprise that she had not mentioned this earlier, the patient maintained that I was interested only in problems, not in successes. I replied that her belief that I was only interested in problems might well reflect the fact that she insisted on relating to me according to the view that I am a domineering, demanding person, despite the absence of supporting evidence to that effect.

At another point, she expressed reluctance to discuss a worry about a friend's health, this time on the ground that I expected her to be strong and uncomplaining. I noted that she seemed to believe I wanted to hear neither about success nor about worries, and that this made me wonder what she thought might be my interest in doing my work?

The patient benefited by the demonstration that her theories about therapy, and about what she anticipated about the therapist's attitudes, might be based on preconceptions, and that they seemed somewhat refractory to revision. She realized that her experience of the treatment was incorrect, and also that this discovery seemed not to modify her ideas and feelings about treatment significantly.

However, the conviction that her attitude in treatment was irrational did lead to her accepting that she evinced certain character traits. They included a defensive attitude that seemed to make learning and adaptation difficult, and a naive childlike stance in relation to putative powerful adults, of whom the analyst seemed to be one, who could confer wealth and other power, but who were demanding and depreciating. In many ways, she could see, this combination of defensive, yet childlike character traits represented her experience as the resentful, covertly rebellious older sister who wished to resist her parents' desire that she defer to her younger brother's needs, while, at the same time, she wished to occupy the indulged brother's preferred place.

While these conclusions had little effect on her behavior, they did influence her in the sense that she became convinced that her romantic and professional life were both restricted because of inner factors, and she entered analysis. Analytic work revealed much about this woman's underlying conflicts. For example, it became apparent that her reluctance to marry had to do with her fear and guilt about her competitive wishes, originally relating to her younger brother, but now directed toward the younger brother substitute, her lover, and toward the potential infant. The character trait of being childlike and put-upon served both as a defense against feared enactment of her incestuous and competitive sibling wishes, and as a punishment for them, and it also allowed for a certain gratification of her hostile, negativistic, ultimately murderous desires.

Her selection of her first husband now appeared to have served her unconscious wishes to avoid the possibility of gratifying her hostile wishes toward a child, who represented both an envied boy competitor and a sibling rival. She had used her husband's attitude as a way of avoiding awareness of her own phobic attitude. She could blame him and feel morally superior, while feeling put upon, a degree of discomfort that assuaged her unconscious guilt over her equally unconscious rivalrous sexual wishes and hostile inclinations toward male brother representatives. Continuing analysis led to the further understanding of some of her phobic attitudes, and to a lessening of their influence on her.

CLINICAL ILLUSTRATION 2

The patient was a thirty-two-year-old man who came for consultation because of depression that followed a failed romance. He was worried that he might never be able to form a permanent relationship. He had had both homosexual and heterosexual relations since adolescence. None of these had endured for more than a few months until a romance developed with a woman coworker a year earlier. An intermittent sexual relation with this woman had gone on for six months. Even though he had to fantasize a large penis to maintain his potency, he felt reassured by this relationship since he hoped he would be able to marry and have a family. However, the woman broke off with him and began to see another man, a superior at work. This precipitated depressed feelings and led to the consultation.

The patient's manner and his description of himself led to the conclusion that he presented the picture of an apprentice. He acted compliant and respectful in the interview. He presented what seemed to be a coherent and full history. His response to questions was cooperative. He was humorous and even entertaining.

He said he would accept any recommendation I made and was prepared to borrow in order to pay whatever my fee might be. He would try to arrange to adapt to my schedule. He was eager to solve his problem. However, he could say little about what he thought his problem might be. He realized there must be something about him that disappointed people; perhaps it was his lack of sustained sexual interest.

The history he presented over a period of some months was as follows. The patient was the younger, by three years, of two brothers. The elder brother suffered from an impulsive behavior disturbance connected with birth anoxia, and had often attacked and hurt the patient throughout early childhood. The patient's father worked for a corporation which frequently moved him from place to place, so that the patient rarely lived in the same community or attended the same school for more than two years, until he was sent to boarding school when he was fourteen. The mother was a painter who spent most of her days at her studio, where she could not be interrupted, leaving most of the care of the children to maids.

The patient professed to believe that he had had a very fortunate childhood, and was lucky to have a gifted mother, through whom he was exposed to culture, and a successful father, who was able to supply all the necessaries and many of the luxuries of life. Further, the patient thought that the brother's difficulties were well handled by his parents, who seemed to devote much attention and money to him, constantly being involved with tutors, therapists, and daily problems.

The only period of unhappiness he recalled was when he went away to boarding school, where he felt extremely lonely and homesick for his mother, whom he had adored. He developed insomnia and gastrointestinal pains. However, he attached himself to an older boy, who introduced him to mutual masturbation and fellatio, and occasionally performed anal intercourse upon the patient, all of which the patient accepted without great enthusiasm, but gratefully, given the fact that the older boy was protective and seemed to care for him. After this boy left the school, the patient become involved in transitory homosexual relationships, mainly with older boys or men, but occasionally, he took what he called the big brother role.

Analysis was undertaken. As the months passed, it became gradually evident that the patient's attitude in the analysis, while polite, correct, and generally cooperative, was also tepid. The patient seemed emotionally uninvolved. Hints that similar attitudes also manifested themselves at work and in his social relationships appeared. For instance, after a party at which a woman seemed attracted to him, the patient dreamed he was a space explorer, far removed from earth. I suggested the interpretation that he seemed to remove himself from human contact in the dream. This was followed by the patient's picking up a homosexual partner for a sexual fling, which I again interpreted as an effort to present himself as independent in the sense of not needing others. Perhaps, I ventured, he had never surmounted his disappointment and anger at his mother, who, he might well have thought, had betrayed and abandoned him when he reached adolescence.

This line of interpretation seemed to have no effect. The patient continued to deal with me in a polite, but mechanical way. As the evidence mounted that the patient was not simply aloof but regarded me as simply a mechanical person, as a kind of robot who would teach him how to live, I could point out how he dehumanized me, and that this attitude toward me was quite critical and angry. This seemed more meaningful to him, and had the consequence that he became aware that he had other views of his parents, and particularly of his mother, besides the cursory idealizing cliches of which he had been consciously aware. He remembered angry and critical thoughts and sadistic wishes toward women, whom he had wanted to seduce, dominate, and abandon, as he had felt treated by his mother.

The patient began to report feeling tearful at the movies, especially over scenes of reunions between children and parent figures, but the attitude he displayed in the analysis altered very little.

In the second year of the analysis, I pointed out to the patient that he displayed no curiosity about me when I made unusual changes; for example, when I canceled or changed scheduled appointments. I reminded him that, by contrast, comparable events in other relationships invariably gave rise to lengthy suppositions, anger, disappointment, and curiosity. He had expressed concern about his parents' health when both had had rather severe upper respiratory infections, but had made no comment when I had displayed the signs of a cold and subsequently canceled several hours. He failed to inform me about an important matter he was engaged in at work until some time later, and when I called this delay to his attention, he lamely explained that he thought I would not be interested. Gradually, it became possible to show him that he maintained an aloofness that might well invite an aloof response in his social and work circumstances, and that this attitude was covertly critical and rejecting of me.

In the third year of the analysis, the patient seemed to respond to my announcement of a vacation by seductively exposing himself in the men's room on his office floor. This was a rather risky behavior given the attitude about homosexuality he thought was prevalent at his office, but he also clearly wondered what my sexual response to him might be. My suggestion was that this behavior might indicate that he did not wish me to leave and wished both to seduce me and to threaten that he might behave even more dangerously in my absence in order to provoke my guilt. He now revealed past fantasies of being dead, so that his mother would be overcome with grief and guilt over having neglected him.

The patient then had a dream in which his brother had an accident in which he lost a finger, and then, fantasies of forcing anal intercourse on me, which took him by surprise, occasioned when I kept him waiting for a few moments. That he wished to control me, to seduce me, and disappoint me and that both sexual and vengeful wishes had been concealed and at the same time gratified by the compliant, apprentice behavior that was designed to enlist me as his prisoner-helper older brother and mother, became clearer and could be more convincingly demonstrated. As a consequence, the patient's emotionality intensified. He came to experience feelings of love, anger, and fears of punishment. Concurrently, his reports of his work life and of his relationships, including his relationship with his family, revealed that he had come to behave in a much more original, independent, assertive, and generally gratifying way.

Conclusion

Both these patients illustrate a not infrequent presenting picture and evolution during the course of therapy. Both entered treatment with little conscious understanding that character traits they believed to be reasonable and logical gratified unconscious sexual and aggressive wishes, unconscious self-restrictions, and unconscious self-punitive trends. Neither patient consciously experienced behavior that they estimated to be irrational, noticed symptomatic limitations, or felt unexplained painful affects. In both cases, irrational elements in their expectations about treatment, and in their attitudes toward the therapist became evident. These transference attitudes, mixtures of behavioral, affective, and ideational contents, and parallels between transference manifestations and behavior outside the treatment situation could be discussed over the course of time. With diligent effort, the evidence these revelations brought forward led to the appearance of signs of unconscious conflict in symptomatic expressions as well as to a sense of conviction and understanding of the unconscious conflicts the behaviors represented. Gradually, more adaptive resolutions of their unconscious conflicts could then be achieved.

CHAPTER 4.

The Uses of Moral Ideas in the Mastery of Trauma and in Adaptation, and the Concept of Superego Severity

(1990). *Psychoanalytic Quarterly*, 59:249–269
The Uses of Moral Ideas in the Mastery of Trauma and in Adaptation, and the Concept of Superego Severity
A version of this paper was presented at a panel entitled "Superego: Too Much? Too Little?," Helen Meyers, M.D., chairman, at a Regional Meeting sponsored by the N.Y., N.J., Pa. Regional Council at Mohonk, New York, May 1988.

ABSTRACT

The power of moral ideas, here equated with superego strength, has been explained in increasingly complex terms over the course of the development of psychoanalysis. At first regarded mainly as useful in opposing oedipal instinctual demands, morality came to be seen also as opposed to aggressive wishes while at the same time capable of gratifying aggressive and libidinal forces. In this paper, I discuss the contribution to the strength of morality that comes from the effects of painful ("traumatic") experiences and from the use of moral ideas for social, adaptational purposes. In addition I consider the possibility that unchanging moral ideas can have changes in function in clinical work. A case is presented to illustrate these points.

Ideas about superego functioning have changed during the course of the development of psychoanalysis. I believe it would be useful to add to our more familiar understanding of morality a greater appreciation of its role in the mastery of certain kinds of trauma and its adaptational use in entering into some varieties of social relationships. Such an emphasis is not intended to supplant our view of superego functioning in respect to instinctual control and socialization, but to expand our clinical understanding of its complexity. In the course of my exposition, I shall also call into question what I regard as obsolete notions about superego severity, particularly references to such simplistic ideas as there being such a thing as too much or too little superego—formulations one still occasionally encounters in clinical discussions.

In the period contemporary with and closely following Sigmund Freud's, analysts thought of the superego as a structure of a certain power and fixity, the heir of the oedipus, incorporating parental injunctions. It could be evaluated as appropriately strong, overstrong, or too weak—or alternately first one and then the other—according to judgments about how much conscious and preconscious suppression and unconscious repression of instinctual drive derivative forces was deemed appropriate. Many thought that analysis consisted in dissolving a transference neurosis that reproduced an infantile neurosis, a process aimed at resolving oedipal conflict. To relieve the patient of some of the excessive pressure of moral injunctions emanating from the superego was regarded as one aspect in achieving the therapeutic aim. Knowledge and the generalizations of psychoanalytic theory about psychopathology and its causes then were not the same as knowledge and theory are now.

An excerpt from Freud's *Outline of Psycho-Analysis* (1940) can serve as a reminder of the way in which Freud preferred to formulate the question near the end of his life.

The picture of an ego which mediates between the id and the external world, which takes over the instinctual demands of the former in order to lead them to satisfaction, which derives perceptions from the latter and uses them as memories, which, intent on its self-preservation, puts itself in defence against excessively strong claims from both sides and which, at the same time, is guided in all its decisions by the injunctions of a modified pleasure principle—this picture in fact applies to the ego only up to the end of the first period of childhood, till about the age of five. At about that time an important change has taken place. A portion of the external world has, at least partially, been abandoned as an object and has instead, by identification, been taken into the ego and thus become an integral part of the internal world. This new psychical agency continues to carry on the functions which have hitherto been performed by the people [the abandoned objects] in the external world: it observes the ego, gives it orders, judges it and threatens it with punishments, exactly like the parents whose place it has taken. We call this agency the super-ego and are aware of it in its judicial functions as our conscience. It is a remarkable fact that the super-ego often displays a severity for which no model has been provided by the real parents, and moreover that it calls the ego to account not only for its deeds but equally for its thoughts and unexecuted intentions, of which the super-ego seems to have knowledge... The super-ego is in fact the heir of the Oedipus complex and is only established after that complex has been disposed of. For that reason its excessive severity does not follow a real model but corresponds to the strength of the defence used against the temptations of the Oedipus complex (pp. 205–206).

Today, influenced by clinical experience and by the thinking of such writers as Anna Freud (1936) about sublimation, Heinz Hartmann about adaptation and change of function (1939a), (1939b), and Charles Brenner (1982) about compromise formation and affect theory, we would not describe the functioning of the superego in quite this way. We would not think that the superego functions exactly like the restrictive parents, simply as a means of taming the instincts, that it is established only after the oedipus complex has been disposed of, or, for that matter, even that the oedipus complex is disposed of. We are less likely to state that some agency is too strong or too weak, or to emphasize fixity, without also adding that even relatively consistent arrangements are plastic and changeable, both in their outward appearance and in the functions they subserve, even when the forms seem to remain unchanged.

This is so primarily because increasing clinical experience has taught us more about the many forces that are involved in constructing psychic arrangements. This increased knowledge has informed us that insofar as the superego is concerned, morality has more sources and uses than those that were emphasized when the structure, superego, was first introduced. I suggest that the judgment about the appropriateness of the strength of moral injunctions be not only based on consideration of defensive needs that oppose oedipal drive derivatives, but also take into account the fact that morality plays a part in response to trauma and in carrying on social relations as well.

Brenner wrote (1982), "Hartmann et al. gave the simplest and most concise definition of the superego. They defined it as the aspect of psychic functioning that has to do with morality" (p. 123). In Brenner's words, "The compromise formations that make up the superego form the basis of the moral aspect of psychic functioning." It is in this sense that I use the term, superego.

A major addition to the understanding of the power of the superego arose with new attention to the problem of aggression. Defense against the temptations of the oedipus complex took on a larger meaning than it originally had, once the vicissitudes of aggressive as well as of libidinal drive derivatives were included under the heading of temptations.

Investigation of patients with depression, negative therapeutic reactions, and self-injuring tendencies led Freud and others to an appreciation of the power of unconscious feelings of guilt and associated wishes for atoning and ingratiation. In the first descriptions, the superego was the structure that arose from the sexual strivings of childhood and their resolution through the creation of moral imperatives that permitted the socialization of the child first in the family and then in the larger social context.

Then, hostile aggressiveness, both innate and consequent to stimulation by humiliation or traumatization, came to be seen as defensively opposed by and at the same time gratified through ethical self-punitive trends. Thus, aggression came to be included as an aspect of the superego (Fenichel, 1928); (Nunberg, 1926) which not only functioned to maintain moral standards in opposition to sexual wishes, but also opposed aggressive wishes and could "sadistically" gratify aggressive inclinations by being "excessively" punitive. Quantitative considerations, in terms of the judgment of "too much morality," were related to the need to counter and gratify powerful aggressive as well as powerful libidinal wishes. Experiences of seduction and frustration increased the intensity of instinctual pressure. "Too much" morality was still ascribed to the superego in some cases.

Another addition to the list of forces influencing the severity of superego pressure was the desire for receptive libidinal gratification. Submission to moral commands could gratify this wish. This was the "masochism" of the ego (Loewenstein, 1957). Despite the growing complexity of the analytic understanding of defensive and instinctually gratifying uses of morality, a certain persisting simplicity of viewpoint still allowed analysts to think in such terms as a conflict characterized by excessively strong defense, or aggression, or harshness of moral force. This was so when other uses of morality besides defense against and gratification of instinctual drive pressures were underemphasized.

One of these additional uses of morality was suggested by Freud (1926) when he wrote, in *Inhibitions, Symptoms and Anxiety*, "the value of the object... is enormously enhanced" (p. 155). Hartmann expanded the importance of this idea. He wrote (1956), "This conception of ego development is at the origin of much of what Ernst Kris... has called 'the new environmentalism' in psychoanalysis. It is the theoretical core for the turning to a closer scrutiny of the impact of object relation on development, and of the ego aspect of object relation, in addition to the earlier consideration of the developmental significance of the libidinal phases" (p. 292). Hartmann felt, with Kris and many others, that observation of the interactions between children and adolescents and their important objects would further clinical and theoretical understanding of development. This renewed interest in object relations led to a greater understanding of the means by which unconscious fantasy, mediated by behavior whose meaning was also unconscious, gratifies and defends against unconscious wishes by enlisting gratifying responses and support for defense from important individuals in the social context.

Hartmann expanded Freud's emphasis on understanding the interrelationship of the biological individual and the sociocultural environment, by including the study of the behavioral manifestations of unconscious aspects of object relations in his considerations. His concept of adaptation made much of the interrelationship between individual and objects, and individual and institutions. Social institutions, like important objects, influence individuals to modify themselves in the service of the interrelationship while at the same time the institutions are available to be used as supports for defense and vehicles for gratification. Hartmann (1939) emphasized the importance of change of function because this idea was central to his concept of adaptation: "The conception of change of function is familiar in psychoanalysis: a behavior-form which originated in a certain realm of life may, in the course of development, appear in an entirely different realm and role. An attitude which arose originally in the service of defense... may, in the course of time... come to serve other functions (adaptation, synthesis, etc.)..." (pp. 25–26).

An example of a form that remains essentially constant when seen as a behavior or in terms of its defensive use, but which undergoes changes in use and meaning over the course of development, is the ethical principle that the strong ought to help the weak. This idea can further the child's wish to enlist the aid of others in support of her or his often painful, unequal struggle with adults. At the same time, this principle reflects personal fantasy and is also a societally accepted belief. In an adaptational sense, it can function as institutions do. The congruence of the societal ideal and the personal wishful ethic makes it possible to use a moral idea to create alliances with objects. This particular idea can be associated with submissiveness, acceptance of mistreatment, and seeking forms of suffering more tolerable than those that are feared, behaviors that subserve internal psychic defensive purposes and drive derivative gratifications. It can also be associated with interpersonal, real-world adaptive aims.

Stein (1981), in writing about the so-called unobjectionable transference, is one who has applied this sort of thinking in examining transference manifestations whose unconscious sources and uses are sometimes overlooked. He found that "normal" character traits, like the desire to work as an analyst, can function as vehicles for the expression of unconscious forces while they serve to permit a seemingly productive analytic process to go forward. Stein's work suggests that shared moral values, like the moral values motivating analysts to treat patients, have an important use in establishing hidden social alliances between analysts and patients.

For example, analysts in training use shared moral values, often unconsciously, to enlist their analyst's sympathies and support. Analysts can be more or less active in permitting or even fostering an unconscious collaboration that uses shared health values as a basis for concealed aims, such as the wish to enlist followers. Often, patients' wishes for approval can be gratified by such alliances, while at the same time, unconscious motives, such as libidinal and aggressive wishes underlying rescue fantasies in both analysand and analyst, escape attention. Such maneuvers can gratify unconscious wishes and, at the same time, protect resistances in both parties. These considerations indicate that "normal" or "unobjectionable" moral standards play a part as forces in inner conflict and in relating to objects as well.

Another of Hartmann's contributions was to point out that adaptive rearrangements go on as life proceeds. Changes in moral ideas and in the number of functions of those ideas are now more likely to be regarded as important in such continuing adaptive psychic changes than they were earlier.

Another emphasis, really a re-emphasis, is that morality can be used in the service of wishes to deny or otherwise overcome experiences of humiliation and helplessness. Mastering trauma (in a broad sense of the term) and painful affects consequent to traumatization should take a more significant position in today's thinking, alongside the mastering of impulses. Becoming like infantile objects by sharing their values, including familial antisocial attitudes, often supports suppression of memories of painful experiences at the hands of the parents or others. Submission, taking on parental moral values as one's own, Loewenstein's (1957, p. 203) "seduction of the aggressor," allows the child to use distress to aid in the mastery of past traumatization by turning passive into active, by magically substituting a provoked lesser injury for the feared one, and by avoiding humiliation by manipulating the feared object. Moral obligations can be used to magically enhance the sense of power by assisting in the denial of past calamities and by practically modifying expected future distress.

Excerpts from a case follow. I hope to illustrate the idea that, in addition to the familiar tendencies toward atoning for morally unacceptable wishes, avoiding feared consequences of instinctual wishes, and gratifying aggressive and libidinal wishes, the less familiar factors, such as I have described above, can also enter into mental constructions involving moral trends. I will omit material regarding the understandings of the use of the moral ideas that are well known in order to be able to concentrate on data that will illustrate those uses I think deserve greater emphasis.

I shall emphasize three main points. One is that in the course of continuing adaptation to the social context, moral ideas change, and unchanged morality acquires changing and added uses. The superego is more plastic than we used to think. The second is that morality gains some of its force from trauma and has an important role in the mastery of trauma. The third is that the use of morality in the service of adaptation, in relating to objects, deserves emphasis. I present the clinical material only to support these points and therefore omit much that was important in understanding the genetic and dynamic development of the patient, his sexual orientation, castration fears and wishes, and other aspects of his psychic organization.

CASE REPORT

A fifty-three-year-old physician entered analysis because of feelings of listlessness and irritation, which he diagnosed as signs of depression. The absence of pleasure and enthusiasm for life of which he complained had appeared intermittently in the past. The presenting episode followed the defeat of a group of colleagues, among whom he was the senior, in a political battle involving patients' rights, an area in which my patient took special interest. The battle had ended with a decision to draw up standards he thought insufficiently protective of the patients who "were not in a position to do for themselves." This outcome had favored the views of other staff members.

Initially, Dr. M responded by becoming angry. He threatened to accept a position in a competing institution which had offered him more than he had where he was, with a conscious idea of "making them sorry," but he permitted himself to be persuaded to stay. Appeals to his sense of loyalty to the institution that, he was told, needed him, some concessions to him, and a guilty feeling about suffering defeat ungraciously entered into this decision.

"To stay or not to stay, that was the question," he said, and he had taken "the easy way out," by acceding to his moral qualms about being vindictive. Other principles, related to ideals about patient care, had been sacrificed. He had accepted a situation that involved material personal sacrifice as well as the humiliation of remaining in a situation where he had been defeated. On the other hand, to devote himself to the interest of others had been a source of deep satisfaction to him in the course of his life, and he hoped it would prove to be so again. Yet, resentful thoughts had not left him, and he said he had come to realize that he had often, as in this instance, suffered unnecessary loss in terms of his own desires because of his moral attitudes. He was unable to understand why it seemed that to benefit others must involve loss to himself. On the surface, his seemed to be a case of too much superego.

The anamnesis revealed that he was the third of three children. A sister, eight years older, had been a disappointment to his mother, who openly complained she had wanted a boy. The patient said the sister played no large part in his current life, except that she made occasional demands, without ever offering him anything in return. He criticized her for having a sense of entitlement without noticing his own tone of mistreatment, or his own sense that doing for others entitled him to a return. While he was aware of his belief that he had a moral obligation to help his sister and believed that he was overly meticulous, to his detriment, in doing so, at this point he was unaware of the great satisfaction he felt in his sense of moral superiority, nor did he recognize the rivalrous feelings that were satisfied through his contemptuous description of her. Further, he was not consciously aware of the implicit invitation he was offering me—to join him in admiring his high principles and in disparaging his sister's character.

A second child, a boy, one and a half years older than the patient, was a difficult infant who later became a violent, impulsive child and often attacked and hurt the patient. The patient remarked that his brother was a needy, sick person, like the parents, for whom he felt he ought to do more. However, his brother spurned his efforts to help, instead treating Dr. M with contemptuous condescension, as he had throughout their lives. The patient continued to present himself as a high-minded, honorable person, superior to both siblings, entitled to, and because he assumed I shared his ideals, likely to get my admiration and respect.

In his early years, the patient was a winning and tractable child, very attached to his mother. He described her as a vain, charming woman, susceptible to periods of withdrawn tearfulness and of outgoing seductiveness, which she exercised in the service of an ambition for social climbing. The patient thought he was used as a vehicle for this ambition, a role which he generally accepted. He accepted his mother's encouragement to perform for her as a tidy, well-behaved, unaggressive child before her friends, by meekly accepting her enrolling him in socially useful dancing classes, summer camps from the age of five, and prep school at the age of eight, and by allowing her to use the connections made by him with the children of socially desirable people to ingratiate herself with what she regarded as higher types.

The father was presented as a successful consulting engineer from a lower-class background, uncultivated, and an embarrassment to Dr. M's mother, but tolerated as a necessary factor because the money he earned made it possible for the mother to pursue her social aspirations.

The father was aloof and distant and absent from home for weeks at a time. The patient could remember no personal contact with him, but could recall feelings of intense resentment and jealousy when his parents went off on vacations, leaving him behind in the care of servants, or when they went out for evenings. He had many memories of sitting and watching his beautiful mother, dressed in underwear, putting on makeup and trying on dresses, and asking his opinion about what she should wear. And he remembered subsequent feelings of anger and loneliness when his closeness with her was interrupted because she went out with father, returned from a trip, leaving him alone with his brother, who then took the opportunity of teasing him and hitting him. These memories dated, in his opinion, from the age of two or three.

A significant change in his manifest personality occurred when he was five. At that time, a nursemaid to whom he was very attached and who, with a family houseman, functioned as an affectionate and undemanding family within his family, married the houseman and left the family's employ. It was later revealed that she gave birth shortly afterward. He had no memories indicating that he knew of her pregnancy or involvement with the man before this time.

Following this loss, the little boy was no longer so charming, enthusiastic, and humorous as he had been. He became withdrawn and had a succession of nightmares in which he was buried alive with no one to help him. A few months later, an uncle, a public health officer who worked abroad, visited. Dr. M began to have ambitions to become a missionary in order to minister to the needs of neglected "savages," just as the uncle had done.

His manner in presenting this history was ingratiating, and he also made it clear that he believed that the strong ought to care for the weaker, that such behavior earned one the right to be treated similarly by others, that others' failure to behave according to his ethical standards deserved to be condemned, and that he was entitled to be rewarded for his high moral intentions. During the initial months of the analysis, as he talked mainly about his work, his colleagues, and his relationships, he continued to manifest a respectful, but covertly demanding attitude. I thought his manner was intended, in the main, to enlist my sympathy and admiration for him, and to influence me to ally myself with him in opposition to those he pictured as mistreaters. I was to minister to him, as he had wished his uncle to do, as he ministered to his patients, the descendants of the "savages," as a reward for his good behavior.

The period of suffering at the age of five came back into focus after the patient saw me driving. He responded by criticizing me for having an expensive car and expressing disappointment that I was not more modest in my personal life and more dedicated to helping others. He complained that the fee was more than he could afford and noted that he himself often charged little or nothing. A brief period of anger with me was followed by aggravated feelings of depression and self-criticism focusing on his own felt insufficiency of concern about patients.

I tried to make him aware of the connection between his moralizing and self-derogation, and his feelings of pain, competitiveness, and resentment, parallel in current life to the situation, now remembered, at age five. He wanted what others had, felt powerless to acquire it for himself, and claimed the right to have more provided for him. When I did not accept and support his right to admiration as the mistreated but morally superior person, he tried to use his goodness to make me feel guilty. His self-criticisms represented self-punishment and also renewed efforts to ingratiate himself with me, or to threaten me, in order to arouse my sympathy and support for his wish to be good.

Feelings of depression persisted. He thought about the many advantages he had had in life, including the possibility of being analyzed, of which he made little use. He apologized for being boring and critical of me, and said that he had felt the same way during other periods of his life.

One such period, which came to occupy his thoughts, was the time when he was sent to boarding school at age eight. Masters had taken an interest in him, but he had not appreciated them. Probably, their attitude toward him was more distant and official than he wished it were and needed it to be. He indulged in masturbation with a fantasy of being adopted by a schoolmate's father, supplanting the schoolmate in his father's affections, and performing fellatio on this man. The need to be thought so good seemed connected to guilt about these sexual and rivalrous wishes. This interpretation had no apparent effect on the course of his ideas.

He continued. He had spent Christmas of that year with this boy's family while his own parents were away on one of their vacations, and had likened himself to Scrooge, who had been abandoned by his parents during a Christmas vacation as a child. His friend's family's reading of *A Christmas Carol* and the happy atmosphere in their home seemed to emphasize his Scroogelike character as it stimulated his resentment of their Cratchit-like happiness, from which he felt excluded.

I related this material to his transference fantasies that I would do more for him if he could either persuade me that he was a good, that is to say, compliant, patient, or if he could make me feel guilty about doing too little to alleviate his distress. He became angry and sullen about one of my vacations, came to sessions late, failed to pay on time, and redoubled his efforts to be a helping person.

On the one hand, he reported a change in his attitude at work. There, he felt happier and more productive and saw that his political activities had been carried out in a provocative and self-defeating way in the past. Now his views seemed to have more influence. On the other hand, he continued to feel very guilty, reported that he seemed to be drinking a great deal, and revealed homosexual activities. I suggested that he continued to wish to show me how good he was and also wanted me to feel responsible for his condition in order to punish me, to elicit affectionate help, and to avoid memories of his past sufferings. This last comment seemed to have the effect of enhancing his capacity to inform me of important feelings and ideas.

The history of his sexuality was now expanded. In adolescence, he had practiced mutual masturbation with a roommate. In college, he had had several sexual relationships with women, by whom he felt used and toward whom he felt guilty because he thought he seduced them without affection or interest in them. After college, he had fallen in love with a man with whom he continued to have a close relationship even after this man's marriage. After his friend's marriage, Dr. M tried to befriend a former professor whom he regarded as an ideal of ethical behavior. When the professor asked him if he were homosexual and made it plain that an intimate relationship with the

73

patient, who desperately wanted to be thought of as a beloved son, was impossible, Dr. M underwent a period of grief and anger. At that juncture his current sexual behavior commenced: he picked up teenage homosexual prostitutes whom he befriended, lent money, and encouraged to become heterosexual. He also made a conscious decision that henceforth he would be self-sufficient and never cry again, as a moral principle. Interpretation continued to focus on the various means he employed to try to avoid painful memories.

He was surprised when his associations turned to his description of his relationship with his mother during and after the period just after college. His homosexual love affair seemed to have followed his discovery that his mother had been hospitalized for a depression. At first, he made efforts to arrange medical care for her but soon realized she preferred his father's care. He suffered a sense of disappointment but did not cry. Three years later, the father died, and the patient then assumed the role of his mother's caretaker, running her household, paying her bills, and managing her investments and medical needs.

Over the course of some weeks I made various interpretations having to do with what I thought I understood at the time. It seemed to me that the father's death had come at about the time Dr. M's lover had married, that his effort to find a new father had represented a response to this event, as much as to the loss of the sexual relationship with the lover, and that his caretaking attitude toward his mother, while continuing a long-standing wish and behavior toward her, also represented a wish to be a woman and mother himself. The patron who disappointed him was to be the father, he, the mother, and his mother, the child. His attitude toward homosexual prostitutes and toward me in the transference now reflected the wish to be fathered and to act as mother, in order to reverse the situation in which he had felt seduced and frustrated by his mother and in order to atone for his guilty wishes about destroying and replacing his brother and father. The continuing effort to distance himself from the painful experiences of his childhood by adopting the missionary, parental role in association with admired others and by attributing the sick, needy, savage qualities to others seemed most important, as did his use of morality to create supportive relationships and assist him in his efforts to see himself as powerful provider.

This interpretation had the effect of producing tears and feelings of great sadness. Over a period of months, the patient reported experiences of grief related to what he now saw as his great feelings of deprivation and loss in connection with both parents. For the first time, their vacations, their sending him to boarding school, his mother's building him up to feel vital and loved but repeatedly demonstrating that she preferred his father, her friends, or her beauty, all appeared to him as deprivations and unbearable losses. His drinking increased as did his manifest rage with me. I was blamed for taking his love for his mother away from him, for leaving him without anyone, and for destroying his belief that at least one element in his sexual behavior, the wish to do good to the prostitutes, reflected only altruism. Further, my interventions had broken his determination not to cry.

I responded in various ways. One was to maintain that it seemed that his morality, his self-castigation for being envious, jealous, and insufficiently altruistic, had served to punish him for the feelings of resentment and destructiveness of which he had been aware, but that they had also had the important function of helping him avoid the experience of feelings of humiliation and helplessness in his past. Another was to ask whether one of the motives for his drinking was to help him suppress his sexual feelings. I suggested that his seemingly moral principle, to place others' interests before his own, enabled him to suppress wishes that he feared.

Subsequent to this work, the patient's associations in the analysis again came to center on events of everyday life. He spoke of his continuing, generally gratifying functioning at work, of the growing appreciation of his administrative ideas among colleagues, of his anticipation of promotion, and about problems with patients with which he seemed generally able to deal to his own satisfaction. However, after a few weeks he began to fall silent for unusual periods of time. He had a confession to make. He had joined a church-associated support-discussion group and was certain that I would disapprove. I might find some way of showing him that this involvement was, as previous involvements had been, something that he would have to give up. He had to confess to an almost sensual feeling of contentment at his meetings where he could reveal his feelings, his strengths, and his weaknesses to others, and accept those that others reported. Perhaps, like his mother, I would reject him if he revealed his pride in himself or his interest in others.

I wondered whether he felt a particular difficulty in revealing the sensual aspects of his feelings, given the fact that he had recently come to be able to feel more satisfaction in his accomplishments and to report his self-satisfaction to me.

He replied that he had a further secret to report. One day I had mentioned feelings of humiliation. He had not understood what I meant. Perhaps the following night, or one night soon after, he had dreamed his mother was alive and young, and he felt attracted to her. As a child, he remembered sexual feelings toward the maid and even toward his mother. The maid had responded in a kindly way, but his mother had shown disgust. He had indeed felt profoundly humiliated and embarrassed but had forgotten these early events until, in adolescence, he informed his mother that he had ejaculated for the first time. She indicated that she wished to hear nothing of this. He again felt humiliated and rejected and suddenly remembered his childhood experience. When he confessed the story to a priest, the priest was shocked and horrified. Guilt about such feelings had followed him ever since. He feared that revealing such feelings to me might lead to similar shock and horror on my part. On second thought, he added, his attitude about sexuality, his own and others', about ethics, and about the behavior of his colleagues had undergone significant change. He no longer thought these sexual, competitive, and possessive desires were so disgraceful.

Not only had his moral ideas changed in becoming less rigid and more related to particular circumstances, but also, he thought, ethical considerations had come to have more to do with questions of what might help others than with uses having to do with assuring himself of his own goodness, independence, and powers. On further consideration, he thought that an element that he wished to discuss, but was hesitant to bring up, was separating from me by terminating the analysis. Now, in discussing this, he thought that, perhaps, no longer being a boy unable to perform like a man, he no longer needed to claim that his desires were evil and selfish because they were doomed to frustration. He added, "The desire of youth had defined what was virtuous." Perhaps now he could consider ending the analysis with less guilt and fear.

DISCUSSION

The history of this patient's character development as it became clearer to him and to me during the course of his analysis reflected continuing change in his moral ideas and in the uses to which he put morality. The preoedipal period had been marked by a seemingly willing compliance with his mother's wish that he be a good boy. Self-critical attitudes did not occur, as far as we know, until after the remembered traumatic disappointment in the maid and the houseman. His morality then seemed to serve his wish to attach himself to his uncle, and his uncle to him, by becoming like the uncle. This method, designed to enlist outside support by emulating parental substitutes who, he hoped, would thereby come to love and foster him, persisted into his adulthood.

It was only later that he began to *use* being good. He used good behavior in such a fashion that compliance was more apparent than actual, in order to punish himself and others. He came to use his guilt to evoke guilt in others and to show his moral superiority in order to make others feel inadequate. Eventually, his sense of moral superiority and entitlement came to result in frustration and disappointment in life. He provoked rejection and suffered its consequences.

His use of moral ideals to establish himself as a superior person also came to be increasingly supported by his desire to avoid conscious memories of loss and humiliation. Successive blows strengthened the forces that supported this purpose. What seemed to be morality to him, others more and more often took to be moralizing. His sense of entitlement made it unlikely that others would deal with him sympathetically. The moral behavior that at first functioned as an appeal to others remained effective as a defense against sadness and sad memories, but later it also become a factor that limited his experiences of satisfaction.

A further revision of the use of the consistent, unchanging idea that the weak are entitled to help from the strong took place during the analysis. Then this idea acquired greater force as a guiding principle, as a satisfiable, gratifying ideal. At the same time, its use for ingratiation, provocation, punishment, and avoidance of painful memories from the past lost some power.

Dr. M did not suffer as a consequence of too much superego. He suffered because he continued to use morality in the service of his wishes to forget, suppress, and revise memories of experiences that could arouse painful feelings of humiliation and helplessness. This method helped him limit his conscious distress but did little to allow him to deal with the underlying sources of his suffering. These remained, despite his defensive efforts. In addition, he suffered because he used moral stances in efforts to gain support for his self-aggrandizing wishes, and to punish and threaten those who did not succumb to his attempts to ingratiate himself. These efforts gratified some wishes and had some adaptive usefulness, but they also brought about rejection and retaliation, just the effects that he wished to avoid and that, in another time, had influenced him in constructing those methods in the first place.

That moral ideas are used to mediate relationships with objects throughout life, and that they undergo changes of function throughout the course of development and during psychoanalysis, is evident in my clinical material. The analytic experience resulted in the appearance of new moral ideas, in further revision of the uses of persisting moral ideas, and in a diminution in some of their uses in this patient.

That morality can be used as a part of defenses against painful ideas of weakness and that it plays an important, often revised, and growing part in relating to the objects through whom sensual and hostile gratification is achieved, is also illustrated by my clinical material.

These observations help us to understand the power of morality, but should not lessen our appreciation of the fact that moral ideas defend against drive derivatives that seem threatening and that they gratify aggressive and libidinal wishes through symbolic means. But I find it helpful to emphasize that both changing and persisting moral ideas have changing functions; they participate in the continuing modulation of one's relation to the social context and help one to modify moods and self-perceptions. When seen as additions to the long-familiar uses of morality, these uses of moral ideas can explain phenomena that were described as consequent to excessive superego strength in the past, when these uses had not yet been sufficiently appreciated.

REFERENCES

Brenner, C. (1982). *The Mind in Conflict*. New York: Int. Univ. Press.

Freud, A. (1936). *The Ego and the Mechanisms of Defence*. New York: Int. Univ. Press, 1946.

Freud, S. (1926). Inhibitions, symptoms and anxiety *S.E.* 20.

——— (1940). An outline of psycho-analysis. *S.E.* 23

Fenichel, O. (1928). The clinical aspect of the need for punishment. In *The Collected Papers of Otto Fenichel*, First series. New York: Norton, 1953 pp. 71–92

Hartmann, H. (1939a). *Ego Psychology and the Problem of Adaptation*. New York: Int. Univ. Press, 1958

——— (1939b). *Psychoanalysis and the concept of health*. In: Essays on Ego Psychology. *Selected Problems in Psychoanalytic Theory*. New York: Int. Univ. Press, 1964 pp. 3–18.

——— (1956). The development of the ego concept in Freud's work In: *Essays on Ego Psychology. Selected Problems in Psychoanalytic Theory*. New York: Int. Univ. Press, 1964 pp. 268–296.

Kris, E. (1950). Notes on the development and on some current problems of psychoanalytic child psychology *Psychoanal. Study Child* 5:24–46.

Loewenstein, R.M. (1957). A contribution to the psychoanalytic theory of masochism. *J. Am. Psychoanal. Assoc.* 5:197–234 .

Nunberg, H. (1926). The sense of guilt and the need for punishment. *Int. J. Psychoanal.* 7:420–433

Stein, M.H. (1981). The unobjectionable part of the transference *J. Am. Psychoanal. Assoc.* 29:869–892.

CHAPTER 5

The Contribution of Hartmann's Adaptational Theory to Psychoanalysis, with Special Reference to Regression and Symptom Formation

(1989). *Psychoanalytic Quarterly*, 58:571–591
The Contribution of Hartmann's Adaptational Theory to Psychoanalysis, with Special Reference to Regression and Symptom Formation

ABSTRACT

My experience of clinical work is consistent with the conclusion that both practice and theory are improved by applying the contributions of Heinz Hartmann. His work provides an important conceptual bridge to understanding the adaptive and pathologic changes that appear in the course of human development. The specific details of those changes are just as much an issue demanding the analyst's attention as is the tracing of patterns of childhood instinctual life. In this paper, I will point to some areas of controversy where renewed attention to Hartmann's ideas might be useful, and I will attempt to illustrate the clinical utility of his theoretical contributions.

Heinz Hartmann is generally acknowledged to be one of the outstanding theoreticians in the history of psychoanalytic thought. The nuclei of his ideas, which he later elaborated, both independently and with his co-authors, Ernst Kris and Rudolph Loewenstein, first appeared fifty years ago in his influential monograph, *Ego Psychology and the Problem of Adaptation*.

In *Group Psychology and the Analysis of the Ego* (1920), *The Future of an Illusion* (1927), *Civilization and Its Discontents* (1930), and other works, Freud had already pointed to connections between individuals› inner psychic arrangements and their social contexts. He applied his analytic understanding to a variety of social questions. Indeed, throughout his work Freud repeatedly demonstrated the psychological linkages between the personal and the social and between everyday phenomena and those considered to be psychopathologic. Freud's formulation of ego psychology (1923) afforded the possibility of explaining and elaborating on these interdependencies and relationships.

Hartmann took up this task in his work, expressing not only the view that psychoanalytic understanding provides explanations of psychopathology, conflict, and symptom formation, but also the view that psychoanalytic theory constitutes a general psychologic theory, one that can account for psychological functioning in all circumstances. Hartmann's expansion of ego psychology, as he understood it, and his elaboration of the meaning and role of adaptation in psychic arrangements represent his efforts to support this view.

Hartmann's work achieved some of the goals to which Freud's discoveries and theoretical generalizations had pointed the way. Among the more significant proposals Hartmann made were: (1) that ego capacities develop and evolve during the course of maturation, largely independent of conflict; (2) that, like drive derivatives, they should be recognized as constitutionally given, and studied more than they have been before; (3) that psychic arrangements reflect the interrelationships of the innate capacities, the drives, and the social context, the conjunction of which not only permits individuals to arrive at individual adaptive arrangements, but also limits their possibilities; and (4) that careful study of the evolution of adaptive arrangements throughout the course of antecedent development is a necessary (though perhaps not sufficient) condition for arriving at an accurate understanding of those psychic arrangements encountered in the clinical situation.

In this paper, I will attempt to indicate what I think Hartmann contributed in his efforts to make psychoanalytic theory into a more comprehensive, general theory, by comparing his emphases with those of Freud, especially the latter's interest in symptom formation (1926), insofar as this was based upon his ideas about regression. I will point to some areas of continued controversy where renewed attention to Hartmann's ideas might be useful. I will briefly discuss how I believe Hartmann's work has influenced the work of Brenner, perhaps our leading present-day exponent of psychoanalysis as a general psychology. I will attempt to illustrate the clinical utility of Hartmann's theoretical contributions with clinical data.

FREUD'S VIEWS OF SYMPTOM FORMATION AND REGRESSION, 1926

Freud discovered that when links between unacceptable unconscious wishes and consciousness are interrupted, conscious experiences of unpleasure are reduced. He proposed that repression, which constitutes the active interruption of such linkages, causes the repressed unconscious contents to lose their power to influence action except under certain circumstances, which is to say, when either increased instinctual pressure or diminished defensive capacity permits some version of repressed contents to return to consciousness.

Further, Freud proposed that repressed unconscious contents remain unaltered until their reappearance, as happens when analytic work unearths them or when other conditions lead to neurotic outbreaks. Under such circumstances, the balance between wish and defense is altered in favor of the power of the wish; regression and a return of the repressed follow; and then symptom formation may subsequently take place. This approach reflected Freud's discovery of the degree to which the past is continued into later life, but it did not satisfactorily deal with how the past and later life differ. Freud's use of the word, transference, was meant to underline the fact that something in the past is carried forward and attached to something in a later contextual frame.

Freud was, to be sure, aware of some problems in this line of thinking. For example, in discussing Little Hans, he wrote (1926) that

the idea of being devoured by the father gives expression, in a form that has undergone regressive degradation, to a passive, tender impulse to be loved by him in a genital-erotic sense... Is it... a question merely of the replacement of the [psychical] representative by a regressive form of expression or is it a question of a genuine regressive degradation of the genitally-directed impulse in the id? It is not at all easy to make certain (p. 105).

By and large, Freud favored the idea that the symptom represents a regressive reactivation, but in any event, an earlier state reappears as a consequence of regression.

Freud went on:

A symptom arises from an instinctual impulse which has been detrimentally affected by repression. If the ego, by making use of the signal of unpleasure, attains its object of completely suppressing the instinctual impulse, we learn nothing of how this has happened. We can only find out about it from those cases in which repression must be described as having to a greater or less extent failed. In this event the position, generally speaking, is that the instinctual impulse has found a substitute in spite of repression, but a substitute which is very much reduced, displaced and inhibited and which is no longer recognizable as a satisfaction. And when the substitute impulse is carried out there is no sensation of pleasure; its carrying out has, instead, the quality of a compulsion... The substitutive process is prevented, if possible, from finding discharge through motility; and even if this cannot be done, the process is forced to expend itself in making alterations in the subject's own body and is not permitted to impinge on the external world (pp. 94–95).

Thus Freud apparently continued to make use of the first anxiety theory, in which he held that repression causes anxiety as a consequence of the "damming-up of libido" (1914pp. 84–86).

Freud provided several ways to account for the appearance of change in the course of development. One explanation proposed that socially acceptable behaviors arise when the suppression of unwelcome wishes brings about a delay of gratification, permitting psychic activity to devise modified, gratifying, sublimated behaviors.

Another change Freud (1926) described is that which results from "a tedious or interminable sequel in which the struggle against the instinctual impulse is prolonged into a struggle against the symptom...

The ego now...makes an adaptation to the symptom...the symptom gradually comes to be the representative of important interests... [secondary gain from illness]" (pp. 98–99). The "adaptation" Freud described was conceived of as a subsequent development and not one that appears coincident with symptom formation. Freud never systematically or extensively addressed the question of how the evolution of the capacity to understand one's inner needs and outer conditions, to enact one's wishes and to anticipate either the advantageous or the doleful consequences of actions, exerts its effects on development.

Freud explained inhibition as a consequence of a need to defer gratification and accept social constraints, and also as a punishment for forbidden unconscious wishes. Behavior that is motivated by the need to avoid the imagined unpleasant consequences of wishes, and that makes use of substituting childlike, passive forms of gratification in order to do so, was said to reflect regressive substitution for, or regressive degradation of, the form in which instinctual wishes emerge. Freud (1920) proposed that severe forms of inhibition, like depression, suicide, and the negative therapeutic reaction, represent the effects of the biological death instinct. The intermediate links by means of which this hypothesized biological determinant was connected to its psychological manifestations were not well described by him.

HARTMANN'S REVISIONS

The essentials of Hartmann's contributions, later elaborated but fundamentally unaltered in subsequent publications (e.g., Hartmann, Kris, and Loewenstein, 1949), were presented in *Ego Psychology and the Problem of Adaptation*.

To briefly summarize the subtle and complex reasoning which characterized Hartmann's work is to do it an injustice. However, it is possible to say that among his chief contributions were the following ideas. (1) Detailed study is required of the interrelationships between thinking on different levels of consciousness and from different periods of development. (2) The maturation of innate capacities needs to be better studied and more thoroughly integrated, in order to enhance our understanding of mental functioning. (3) The capacity to anticipate is particularly important. (4) Mental functioning should be looked at to a greater degree in terms of its adaptational interdependency with the social context.

He recommended that analysts should be more attentive to the changes of function consistent with the maturation that psychic arrangements undergo in the course of adaptational development throughout all phases of life. The individual's understanding of and relationship with the environment from the standpoint of its offering possibilities for adaptational solutions should also be a central interest.

Taken together, these ideas represent a considerable change from Freud's point of view, which concentrated on intrapsychic conditions and emphasized the contextual and adaptational dimensions less, which regarded symptoms and their sequelae as special psychopathological formations that are constructed only after repression and regression have occurred, and which maintained that repressed wishes are not gratified in everyday interactions with the social context.

Hartmann (1939) wrote that "psychoanalytic ego psychology... is, and will be, increasingly interested in the details of behavior, in all the shadings of conscious experience, in the rarely studied preconscious processes, and in the relationships between the unconscious, preconscious, and conscious ego" (p. 6). He implied that Freud's attention had not always adequately focused on such linkages.

In addition to recommending that more attention be paid to the details of behavior in the various developmental phases and to the relationships between the levels of consciousness, Hartmann pointed out that we ought to pay attention to "the development outside of conflict of perception, intention, object comprehension, thinking, language, recall-phenomena, productivity, to the well-known phases of motor development, grasping, crawling, walking, and to the maturation and learning processes implicit in all these and many others" (p. 8). He wrote: "What we do not yet have is a systematic psychoanalytic knowledge of... reality-fears" (p. 9), "of special talents" (p. 10), of the relations between "constitution, maturation of the apparatus, and learning processes" and "those libidinal processes, identifications, endogenous and exogenous (instinctual drive and environmental) factors which may lead to conflicts and to disturbances of function" (p. 11).

Hartmann placed particular emphasis on the importance of anticipation. He wrote about the "*function of anticipating* the future, orienting our actions according to it and correctly relating means and ends to each other. It is an ego function and, surely, an adaptation process of the highest significance. We may assume that ego development enters this process as an independent variable, though naturally the ego function involved may secondarily yield pleasure» (p. 43).

Hartmann's stress on the need to consider the consequences of maturation is further reflected in the following: "... we must also keep in mind the phenomenon of 'change of function,' the role of which in mental life and particularly in the development of the ego seems to be very great... The conception of change of function is familiar in psychoanalysis: a behavior-form which originated in a certain realm of life may, in the course of development, appear in an entirely different realm and role" (pp. 25–26).

In addition, Hartmann recommended considering change in the environment in tandem with change in function. "It is often overlooked that the degree of need gratification and particularly the possibilities for development afforded by a given social order may not have parallel influences on the child and on the adult" (p. 32).

In Hartmann's point of view, the concept of regression commands less importance than it had in Freud's view. Regression is one of many phenomena, all of which ought to be considered in the context of the level of development of the individual concerned, as well as in the context of his or her experiential and maturational history. One should also take into account that an individual's environment is both perceived differently and responds quite differently to him or her as he or she continues to grow, develop, and mature, in comparison to the way it did in the person's past.

VIEWS OF LATER CONTRIBUTORS

Peter Blos (1962) has added much to the understanding of adolescence. Blos often cited Hartmann as one who had encouraged him in his interests, for instance in quoting Hartmann's suggestion that "the potentialities for formation of personality during latency and adolescence have been underrated in psychoanalytic writing" (p. 11).

For example, Blos (1965) discussed the significance of the intensification of passive wishes and the consequent return to a hypothesized primal passivity in adolescence. He noted the difficulty adolescents generally have in lessening their childhood attachments to their parents, and their problems associated with reliving oedipal conflicts and disappointments. Blos also pointed out that regression in adolescence brings with it progressive possibilities, by way of "regression in the service of the ego," an idea also important to Hartmann. These ideas have been generally accepted.

Nevertheless, it seems to me that Hartmann's belief that we ought to place more emphasis on ego development in the adolescent period has not been followed with sufficient vigor. Adolescents become aware of their new capability to bring about in reality both destructive and sexual ends, which they had been unable to do more than wish for earlier. The possibility of causing pregnancy, of abandoning lovers and others, of causing physical injury, the awareness of the presence of new powers and of greater opportunities for success as well as for failure, all enter into adolescent conflict and adaptation in important, perhaps insufficiently appreciated ways. The case I summarize below illustrates this point.

Mahler was also encouraged in her interest in observing young children by Hartmann's views. She was especially interested in investigating problems relating to psychosis and those concerning the later effects of separation-individuation phase difficulties. She attempted to distinguish between the psychotic regression of the autistic or symbiotic child and the regression of more normal people. Mahler (Mahler and Furer, 1968) wrote:

Several formulations about infantile psychosis center around the idea that these pathological formulations represent regressions to very early, yet normal phases of development... The pathological formations, however, whether they are predominantly autistic or symbiotic syndromes, represent grave distortions that take place by way of a pathological intrapsychic process... that is, regression in the sense of a psychotic defensive regression of intrapsychic formations [to

92

a pre-existent psychotic state] ... the psychotic child [does not regress] to any known phase of development (pp. 54–55).

Instead,

the pathological regression in psychosis involves a return to the earliest level of preobject and part-object relationships ... (p. 228).

To what extent regression is a useful concept in understanding psychotic states remains an issue for debate. Willick (1989) has recently argued that many severely ill persons display conditions involving deterioration of cognitive functions that had developed normally and had never been defective in the past. Willick suggested that the main cause might well be a biological one, as is the case in Huntington's disease, and that no return to a hypothesized previous psychological state is involved.

Mahler's discoveries about infantile development are often misused by the inexperienced—and sometimes by the experienced as well. For instance, a clinician may observe adult reactions to separations and conclude that the adult problems can be explained as re-editions of difficulties from the separation-individuation phase. In such cases, as with efforts to explain psychotic phenomena or in connection with issues involving focal cognitive difficulties (Kafka, 1984), more emphasis on the role of ego maturation and adaptation and more accurate definition of developmental linkages would, in my opinion, lead to more precise conclusions.

Modell (1968), (1988), Loewald (1960), (1978), Anzieu (1983), Basch (1988), and Ornstein (1988) are among respected psychoanalytic contributors who place great emphasis on regression as a factor in their theoretical orientations, and whose views, often in disagreement with Hartmann's, contribute to the continuing dialectic that Hartmann, to a great degree, brought about.

BRENNER'S EXTENSIONS OF HARTMANN'S VIEWS

As Hartmann extended the scope of Freud's formulations of a general psychology, so Brenner has extended Hartmann's legacy. Brenner's contributions have emphasized the ever-present influence exerted by infantile drive derivatives. He has suggested that these drive derivatives, together with defensive and superego forces, are invariably represented in every psychic formation throughout life.

Thus, symptoms, character traits, actions, the superego, and many, if not all, other aspects of mental life of interest to psychoanalysts are to be understood as compromise formations. In this, he went beyond Hartmann's reformulation.

Brenner (1982) wrote:

The available psychoanalytic evidence indicates that what has been and is repressed does have access to consciousness, even when repression is successfully maintained ... Id impulses, including repressed ones, exert an influence on conscious psychic functioning and on behavior, although their tendency to do so is opposed by the ego's defensive activity (p. 113).

Brenner also wrote that compromise formations take into account the need to maintain important relationships that both provide gratification and contribute to instinctual restraints. As Hartmann had noted, social institutions can be essential in helping individuals to restrict impulses; religion and mourning rituals are examples of such organized aspects of the social environment that interact with individuals' unique tendencies toward compromise formation in the service of adaptation.

CLINICAL ILLUSTRATION

The following case example is presented to illustrate that Hartmann's contributions are clinically useful and that some of the data that arose from the patient's several analyses support the general validity of Hartmann's ideas. The material is condensed and incomplete, and conceals or omits many important aspects.

I hope to show the usefulness of applying what I have summarized as Hartmann's views: (1) a correct understanding of the patient required attending to the effects of changes in ego capacities in the course of their maturation; (2) the interrelationships of the patient's capacities, drives, and social contexts both limited the patient in some ways and also accounted for his adaptive arrangements; (3) attention to and understanding of the evolution of this patient's adaptation, especially his adolescent development, was necessary for the accurate and helpful understanding of his psychic arrangements as they appeared during the analysis; and (4) it was important to find the connections that revealed the unity and consistency as well as the changes that appeared in the evolution of this individual's life.

The patient was a professional who entered a third analysis in his fortieth year. He was successful in his work by the community's standards, but not by his own. He was reasonably happily married and had three children. Of two previous analytic treatments, the first, which lasted a year and a half, had not been helpful, and the second, of six years' duration, had been helpful but incomplete. He continued to feel insufficiently successful at work, and he suffered periods of depression, with feelings of inadequacy and failure.

He reported that similar complaints had led to his first attempt at analysis. At that time, he had doubts about his ability, felt childlike, thought he was performing inadequately in his profession, and had periods of depression and anxiety, with insomnia and outbursts of anger. He thought this threatened his career and marriage. He sought out a prominent analyst who was widely respected as an academic and as an administrator.

He said that he began that analysis with anxiety and enthusiasm, fearful that he might not succeed as a patient, but he felt that he had been able to talk reasonably freely. Several months of that analysis were spent in relating his history and current difficulties and in explaining his relationships with the people in his life. During this period, the analyst, he said, made little response, but seemed interested in listening and could understand the patient's feelings and ideas.

The patient reported that a difficulty arose when he overheard the analyst talking angrily on the telephone, evidently to an unsatisfactory employee whom the analyst fired at the end of the conversation. The patient became anxious, told the analyst what he had overheard, wondered what infraction the former employee might have committed, and expressed fear that he might also be found deficient and dismissed as a patient.

The analyst asked the patient to discuss what historical antecedents might have been connected with this reaction. The patient concluded that the analyst subscribed to the theory the patient had gleaned from reading psychoanalytic works, that is, that current difficulties simply represent continuations of earlier ones, and he related a number of memories having to do with infractions of rules he had committed at various times in the past, to which his father, mother, and teachers had responded with punishments.

Among such childhood transgressions, he recalled being discovered by his second grade teacher fighting with a classmate. He reacted to this event by lying, insisting that he had been the good one who had sought only to defend himself from the other's attack. (This behavior, claiming to be the good victim, remained part of this man's repertoire thereafter.) He failed to avoid punishment and was kept after school. His parents found out and were angry and disappointed with him. Other infractions brought a similar result. The parents said something like, "You're a bad boy; you'll never amount to anything," and the patient felt humiliated, guilty, and contrite but also angry and rebellious.

The analyst did not note the hesitancy the patient felt about continuing to explore the "realistic" thoughts of fear and anger he had in respect to the analyst, and consequently, the links between these childhood memories and current transference conditions were not elucidated. A week or so later, the analyst became ill with what the patient later learned was a life-threatening ailment. This caused a three-month interruption in the treatment.

Upon the analyst's return, the patient found it difficult to talk. He worried about the analyst's health, tried to behave in a way he thought cooperative, suppressed growing doubts about the analyst's responsiveness, which he attributed to the analyst's preoccupation with his own health, and began to consider moving to another city. The significance of health questions in the patient's current life was not pursued; therefore, no comparison with earlier theories and impressions could be made.

At one point, the patient's anger erupted. He attacked the analyst by talking disdainfully about the analyst's native city and what he assumed was his lack of cultivation, to which the analyst responded that many people, himself included, regarded this background as quite satisfactory. The patient took this remark as a defensive, angry rebuttal. He became consciously more fearful of the analyst, and withheld the information that he thought the analyst also feared him. Subsequently, he reported only on everyday life. Dreams were not remembered, and a stalemate developed. Eventually, the analyst suggested that the patient might be unanalyzable, or at least unanalyzable by him, and the treatment ended.

A year later, the patient found a second analyst. He felt that this treatment went relatively well. The new analyst interpreted much of the difficulty with the first analyst as having to do with the patient's feelings of desertion during his mother's pregnancy and following the birth of his sibling. This reconstruction evoked painful feelings of loneliness and memories of often unsuccessful efforts to be good. Subsequently, the patient recalled feelings of fear and anger that had followed a newly recovered memory of an episode of illness his mother developed. His own health concerns were found to have developed in part under the influence of his disappointed wish to have an important role with his ill mother. Illnesses reminded him of his humiliation when he had felt unimportant to his mother, and he feared the punishments and further humiliations he might experience if he expressed his anger and its associated wishes to hurt her.

Conflicts over his ambivalent wishes toward his mother throughout latency and adolescence continued to affect the patient and later entered into problems he had in his professional life. Interpretations that his anger against his mother had to do with his earlier feelings of rejection by her led to discussion of his guilt about rivalrous feelings toward his less successful younger sibling. He also achieved a partial understanding of an oedipal period phobia which had involved competitive wishes toward and fears of his father, and frustrated longings to be the most important one to his mother. Similar conflicts had influenced his behavior with the first analyst. The childhood phobia had given way mainly to "goody-goody" behavior and to acting the role of the victim in the attempt to ingratiate himself and to avoid punishment.

A particularly significant piece of work during the second analysis was reported as having taken place around a dream in which the patient, as a child, was taken to see the first analyst by his parents, who asked the analyst to forgive the patient. Interpretations had explained that the patient's wish to deny his hostile feelings toward the analyst for having been sick had been expressed by representing him as healthy and powerful in the dream. The patient's wish to be close to his mother and father and his wish to be forgiven by his parents and helped by them, even though he felt he had been neglectful of his mother during her illness, were seen to have been gratified by their appearing affectionate in the dream. His wish to disavow responsibility for the effects of his provocation of the first analyst was supported by the representation of himself as a child, dependent upon others and thus not responsible.

The patient did something unusual for him: he complained that the analyst seemed unsympathetic and never commiserated with him or explicitly acknowledged how much he had suffered. The analyst commented that the patient wished to be consoled as though he were still a child when, in fact, the analyst would be less than respectful if he failed to point out that the patient was actually a capable adult. At this point, the patient was not able to pursue the question the analyst raised for his consideration, which is to say, why it was that he wished to see himself and to be treated as though he were immature.

The patient told the analyst that significant symptomatic improvement had led him to begin thinking about termination. His desire to terminate was also motivated by a conscious wish to avoid the reappearance of further painful memories. Further, he wanted to prove himself as an adult. He believed his fear of disappointment and failure could be overcome if he broke away from the dependence he felt in analysis and struck out on his own. He was, however, unable to set a date.

The analyst suggested that a basis for the patient's hesitancy in coming to a decision about termination was that he was achieving some gratification by toying with the analyst, just as he might have offered and withheld stool in childhood. The patient responded by feeling convinced that it was time for him to grow up and control his childlike behavior. He was confirmed in his decision to give up his "passivity." He set and kept a termination date.

Some years later, an intense version of the earlier symptoms, all of which had been much relieved during the second analysis, re-emerged. The patient entered the third analysis.

Initial discussion of the previous termination led to the understanding that one motivation the patient had had for wanting to appear childish at that time was to conceal his wish to hurt his analyst by leaving him, once he had progressed to the point where he felt able to do so. Becoming more adult meant having the capacity to carry out vengeful acts that had been long desired but impossible to enact.

The emphasis in the analytic interpretations, different from those which the patient reported as having been more common in the past, came to be more on his fear of causing real damage and provoking retaliation as a consequence of acting on his wishes, rather than on his fear of helplessness and humiliation.

It soon became apparent that rivalrous feelings toward those colleagues who were succeeding socially and professionally were playing an important part in intensifying his conflicts over his own ambitions. Performance anxiety and self-critical thoughts were seen to be punitive consequences of the patient's fear of the imagined destructive effects of his wishes to outdo others. Interpretation of the impact of past narcissistic humiliations in increasing his hostile wishes, together with demonstration of his enhanced present capacity not only to cause harm, but also to find other means of satisfaction, led the patient to accept that he was not as dangerous as he had believed himself to be.

Discussion of what the patient regarded as his realistic capacities to harm his analyst by terminating, his children and wife by neglecting them, and his colleagues by outdoing them now became central.

A period of impotence in adolescence that had followed a sexual relationship in which the patient thought he had impregnated his partner came up in the analytic material for the first time. This experience was seen as a transition between childhood, with its sense of impotence, and adulthood, with its awareness of the possible consequences of potency.

The pregnancy he thought he had caused was retrospectively seen by him as having confirmed his assessment that he had a new, strong, destructive potential. He had thought that an abortion might have to be arranged, with possible danger to the woman as well as destruction of the potential child. This situation was unconsciously linked with a past one in which he had wished to harm, or even kill, his younger brother. The childhood wish to impregnate his mother and kill his brother could now be gratified, albeit in a displaced form and one involving innocent victims. The potency disturbance in adolescence, his performance anxiety in the present, and his restraint in attempting to be good in his analyses were seen as having to do with his fear of the consequences, given his adult capacities, should he act on his childhood wishes.

The patient believed that various actions, whether actually performed or merely planned, had caused actual harm. He thought that in his adolescence he had been successful in humiliating his father through personal attacks that led his father to lose control of himself and act punitively toward the patient. His attacks on the previous analysts had reproduced the earlier situation insofar as he had gratified his rage and satisfied his need for punishment—through provoking dismissal in the first case, and by arranging a not quite optimal termination in the second. The attacks had differed from the earlier attacks on his father in that they also had advantageous aspects; in the first analysis, he was, in fact, able to release himself from an unhelpful treatment, while in the second analysis, he was freed to apply his energies and time in other productive ways.

The immediate precipitant that came to be understood as having led to his entering the third analysis was an increase in the inhibition caused by his rage against his children, who were getting everything that he had not gotten from his own parents. The demonstrated reality of his capacity to lose his temper with or neglect his children influenced him to behave in a good, relatively harmless, though withholding, self-punitive, and somewhat childish manner.

Earlier symptomatic episodes, such as his adolescent depression when he thought he had impregnated his girlfriend and his childhood oedipal, depressive, goody-goody period, were compared with the present version. Other current variants of this pattern were also explored, including his hostile and self-defeating interactions with his siblings and colleagues and his attempts in the transference to be a good, compliant, childlike, but also obstructive, punishing, and self-defeating patient.

The choice of seemingly powerful, healthy analysts came to be understood partly as an effort to reassure himself that he would be unlikely to be able to outdo them or hurt them. The patient realized that he had come to believe that his analysts were angered by his competitiveness and youthful virility and that they could be significantly harmed if he were to fail to improve and then desert them.

The patient came to be convinced that his passive and submissive tendencies had originally developed out of desires to please important adults and thus assure himself of their love and care, and that later, when he came to realize, albeit unconsciously, that he had developed the capacity to put his earlier egoistical and vindictive fantasies into successful action, the same character traits were used by him to conceal his potency.

DISCUSSION

This case illustrates not only the unity and consistency but also the changes of function that the patient's trait of being good reflected during the course of his development, his analyses included. The adaptive, gratifying, and defensive factors that influenced the trait were revealed in their consistencies as well as in their maturational alterations. Both linkages and contrasts were revealed, for instance, in relating the patient's oedipal period adaptation, his latency adjustment, his adolescent experience, and his adult relationships with family, colleagues, and analyst. Common strands were woven through the various stages. His sexual wishes, directed in childhood toward his mother, in adolescence toward girls, in adulthood toward his wife, were associated throughout with wishes to outdo others, including his father, brothers, other men, colleagues, his children, and his analysts, which presents a consistent conflictual picture. Thematic similarities could be described in connection with the childhood attack on a schoolmate rival for his teacher's approval, the adolescent abortion question, the transference complications, and many other situations. Harmful wishes, fears, and being good as a compromise consequence were thematically connected and consistent. To clearly bring out those differences that were consequences of the varied contextual possibilities and of the developmental level of innate capacities, which influenced the patient's ability to understand his wishes as well as his social environment, was also important. The simplistic use of lying in a wishful effort to present an appealing reality in childhood was contrasted with the latency development of the ingratiating character trait of being good; it was also contrasted with adolescent solutions involving conscious decisions and symptoms, as well as with the transferential attempts to use the analyst as disciplinarian, teacher, and gratifier on various levels. In each instance, the consistencies and the changing influence of changing realities and reality evaluations were discussed. The defensive and adaptive changes that were a consequence of cognitive maturation and of changes in the response of the social context strongly influenced the changing aspects of the adaptive arrangements.

In the third analysis, discussing the changing capacity to actually do injury and to achieve sexual and other satisfactions during and after adolescence was particularly in focus. Although patterns of wishes, superego demands, and conflicts that had appeared in the earlier analyses were further elucidated and elaborated, the attention paid to the development of the patient's actual powers to think, to anticipate, and to enact was particularly important in engendering a level of understanding and conviction about himself that he had not achieved earlier.

The case also illustrates the importance of elucidating the connections between unconscious wishes and anticipations, to "reconstruct upward" toward current reality concepts, in the phrase coined by Hartmann's collaborator, Loewenstein (1957), as well as downward toward what was real in the past and what was part of infantile wishful fantasy life. It illustrates as well the capability that compromise formations have to gratify a number of hidden wishes, while simultaneously participating in a variety of adaptive connections with an always vitally present social context.

I should add that I believe that re-examination of Hartmann's ideas may also help resolve some other active controversies, such as the problem of psychotic symptom formation and some of the difficulties over the theory of therapeutic action, although those topics are beyond the scope of this paper.

REFERENCES

Anzieu, D. (1983). *The Group and the Unconscious*. London: Routledge & Kegan Paul.

Basch, M.F. (1988). How does treatment help? A developmental perspective In *How Does Treatment Help? On the Modes of Therapeutic Action of Psychoanalytic Psychotherapy*, ed. A. Rothstein. Madison, CT: Int. Univ. Press, pp. 127–135

Blos, P. (1962). On Adolescence. A Psychoanalytic Interpretation New York: Free Press.

——— (1965). The initial stage of male adolescence *Psychoanal. Study Child* 20:145–164

Brenner, C. (1982). *The Mind in Conflict*. New York: Int. Univ. Press.

Freud, S. (1914). On narcissism: An introduction. *S.E.* 14.

——— (1920). Beyond the pleasure principle. *S.E.* 18.

——— (1921). Group psychology and the analysis of the ego. *S.E.* 18.

——— (1923). The ego and the id. *S.E.* 19.

——— (1926). Inhibitions, symptoms and anxiety. *S.E.* 20.

——— (1927). The future of an illusion. *S.E.* 21.

——— (1930). Civilization and its discontents. *S.E.* 21.

Hartmann, H. (1939). *Ego Psychology and the Problem of Adaptation*. New York: Int. Univ. Press, 1958.

——— Kris, E. & Loewenstein, R.M. (1949). Notes on the theory of aggression. *Psychoanal. Study Child* 3/4 9–36.

Kafka, E. (1984). Cognitive Difficulties In Psychoanalysis. *Psychoanal. Q.* 53:533–550

Loewald, H.W. (1960). On the therapeutic action of psychoanalysis. In *Papers on Psychoanalysis.* New Haven: Yale Univ. Press, 1980 pp. 221–256.

——— (1978). Instinct theory, object relations, and psychic structure In *Papers on Psychoanalysis.* New Haven: Yale Univ. Press, 1980 pp. 207–218

Loewenstein, R.M. (1957). Some thoughts on interpretation in the theory and practice of psychoanalysis In *Practice and Precept in Psychoanalytic Technique. Selected Papers by Rudolph M. Loewenstein.* New Haven: Yale Univ. Press, 1982 pp. 123–146

Mahler, M.S. & Furer, M. (1968). *On Human Symbiosis And The Vicissitudes Of Individuation. Infantile Psychosis.* New York: Int. Univ. Press.

Modell, A.H. (1968). *Object Love And Reality. An Introduction To A Psychoanalytic Theory Of Object Relations.* New York: Int. Univ. Press.

——— (1988). On the protection and safety of the therapeutic setting In *How Does Treatment Help? On the Modes of Therapeutic Action of Psychoanalytic Psychotherapy* ed. A. Rothstein. Madison, CT: Int. Univ. Press, pp. 95–104

Ornstein, P.H. (1988). Multiple curative factors and processes in the psychoanalytic psychotherapies In *How Does Treatment Help? On the Modes of Therapeutic Action in Psychoanalytic Psychotherapy* ed. A. Rothstein. Madison, CT: Int. Univ. Press, pp. 105–127.

Willick, M.S. (1989). Psychoanalytic Concepts of the Etiology of Severe Mental Illness Presented to the New York Psychoanalytic Society, May 9.

CHAPTER 6

Cognitive Difficulties in Psychoanalysis

(1984). *Psychoanalytic Quarterly,* 53:533–550.
Cognitive Difficulties in Psychoanalysis

ABSTRACT

The author raises a number of questions about cognitive difficulties in relation to psychoanalysis. He presents the case of an adult patient in whom previously unrecognized childhood cognitive difficulties were discovered during the course of analysis. Their relationship to the patient's problems in adulthood is discussed. Some suggestions and speculations about the questions raised are presented with the hope of stimulating further exploration of what the author considers to be an interesting and important subject for psychoanalysis.

Certain individuals manifest unusual cognitive characteristics in childhood. These include exceptional abilities in one or another area—in musical or mathematical talent, for example—as well as special disabilities. Often they occur in mixtures. Dyslexia, minimal brain dysfunction, learning disorder, and hyperactivity are among the terms that workers in fields other than psychoanalysis have applied to childhood conditions in which particular cognitive difficulties or combinations of them are prominent. In recent times, psychologists, educators, neurophysiologists, and workers in other disciplines have become increasingly interested in aspects of the general subject. Formerly, the cognitive difficulties of individuals went unrecognized more often than they now do. My clinical experience has been that people with such idiosyncrasies appear fairly frequently as patients. Their cognitive difficulties, whether they had been recognized in childhood or not, play a significant part in adult analyses and therapy, both through their effects on development and, if they persist, through their continuing effects in adulthood. With the exception of some work of Victor Rosen (1955), (1961) and Annemarie Weil (1978), however, little else dealing with the subject has appeared in the psychoanalytic literature.

This paper is presented with the hope of encouraging greater psychoanalytic interest in and discussion of this subject. I wish to raise a number of questions that have occurred to me in the course of working with such patients. For some of these questions I can suggest partial answers, based on my experiences, and for some, I cannot, but I hope that others may become interested in reporting their findings and ideas.

1. What traces of cognitive difficulties that appear in childhood but go unrecognized may persist into adult life, and how can they be discovered in analyses? How can cognitive difficulties that first occurred in childhood and may have persisted into adult life be detected in analyses when the patient is unaware of their presence?

2. What can we learn about the effects of such problems on the development of individuals?

3. How do these problems influence patients as analysands?

4. Do such problems require modifications of analytic technique, or alterations of emphasis or modes of communication, in adult analyses?

5. Can analytic data increase our understanding of the sources of such cognitive idiosyncrasies, or are we limited to achieving

understanding of their specific psychological meanings in the childhood conflicts and psychological development of affected persons?

6. Why has the question received so little attention in the psychoanalytic literature?

By way of orientation, I will summarize what the common manifestations of cognitive "deficits" are thought to be by nonanalysts. I will briefly interpolate one view of some characteristic dysfunctions; this is taken from the extensive review of the subject by a child psychiatrist, Paul Wender. In his book, *Minimal Brain Dysfunction in Children*, Wender (1971) writes, "The principal abnormalities of motor function are... a high activity level and impaired coordination" (p. 13). "A few children are hyperactive and listless." A typical history is of a "clumsy, inept child" (p. 14), perhaps with "poor fine motor coordination," and "difficulty in learning to throw and catch a ball... Shortness of attention span and poor concentration ability are common" (p. 14). There is often "an inability to organize hierarchically so that all aspects of a percept or an idea are of equal importance," which may lead to "an obsessive quality." There are associated learning difficulties. The most serious learning difficulty is "learning to read (although problems in writing, generally sloppiness, and problems in comprehension and arithmetic may be present as well)" (p. 16). Wender writes that, "working with Swedish teenage dyslexics of normal intelligence, Frisk [and co-workers] found that approximately one-third to one-half showed current distractibility and restlessness, sleep disturbance, or impaired motor abilities, and that as children they had had an increased prevalence of speech difficulties, clumsiness and enuresis" (pp. 16–17). Such children often have "low frustration tolerance" and "impulsivity, poor planning and judgment," "defective control." They are often "obstinate" and "controlling." Wender does not note that right-left confusion is a frequent concomitant phenomenon.

I will continue by presenting a case report of an analysis of a patient who manifested a number of these characteristics as a child and as an adult, and who did not become aware of some of them or of their consequence until they were described in his treatment.

Mr. R.'s internist referred him to a consultant, a psychoanalyst colleague, for evaluation of a potency disturbance that the internist could not explain. He came thence to me. He had been married three years to a woman five years younger. His sexual symptom, he told me, was an exaggerated version of a life-long difficulty. It consisted of a lack of interest in intercourse and frequent loss of erection or premature ejaculation on those approximately monthly occasions when he and his wife attempted intercourse. This situation had become increasingly severe over the year preceding his coming to treatment. He had had a life-long anxiety about performing sexually before meeting his wife. His earlier sexual activity had consisted mainly of masturbation. He had had two affairs of several months each and many "one-night stands," more or less successful, before meeting his wife. During the year of courtship and the first year of his marriage, he felt he "performed"—his word—successfully enough to satisfy himself and, by and large, his wife as well, although she informed him that he was inhibited and less pleasing than any of her previous lovers.

The patient connected his idea that he "performed," when I asked him what he meant in using this term, to a notion he often had that he was a "faker," that there was something "not genuine" about him, as if he "pretended" that he had abilities he really lacked in the sexual sphere and in other areas, but he could not be more specific about what he meant. Despite a certain feeling of anxiety and humiliation, things went fairly well until his wife developed pneumonia. He was fearful about approaching her sexually during and for some months after her recovery and felt somewhat less aroused by her after they resumed more frequent intimacy.

More recently, probably when Mrs. R. began to indicate a wish to have a child, Mr. R. noticed that he had less sexual interest in her than before and that he also began to experience periods of irritability, an increased difficulty in getting his work done, and embarrassing mental lapses. He came late to work appointments, misfiled papers, "forgot" names, and neglected to pay bills. His work situation was at that time a cause of considerable anxiety to Mr. R. He was an executive in a large paternalistic advertising corporation with the responsibility for evaluating future directions in which his company might go, as well as for planning administrative structures. The company was doing badly, his advice was not followed, and he felt he was not well regarded. His "Guru," the man who had hired him, had lost influence and seemed on the verge of being let go. If he lost his "Guru," he would risk being exposed as a "faker"; he would feel "lost" himself because he would be "found out" as one who could not "find his way" by himself. Mr. R. felt fearful about his future prospects, especially so since he had distinguished himself neither in selecting his three previous jobs— two of the companies had gone out of business—nor in his own work accomplishment. He had the tendency to begin jobs with energy and enthusiasm and then to become bored, inefficient, and unproductive. He lost interest. Sometimes, he had "superior" ideas and insights he could not clearly communicate to others. Difficulty organizing his ideas in logical sequence impaired his ability to write, slowed him, and added to his work problems. In addition, he felt guilty about his superiority, but mortified when it was unappreciated.

The past history was as follows. The patient was the elder of two children, with a sister four years younger. The mother had been the youngest of three sisters. Mr. R.'s maternal grandfather had become reasonably successful as an engineer, and his mother admired him greatly. This grandmother died when Mr. R.'s mother was in her early twenties. Her older sisters were married, and she cared for her father, keeping house for him until he died suddenly when she was in her mid-thirties. She received a modest inheritance, and shortly after her father's death, married the patient's father, a man eight years younger, who had separated from his family when he emigrated from Europe. After a period of infatuation, she quickly became disappointed in her husband. His defects, she thought, were that he was uncultured and uninterested in becoming more cultured, and that he was a drinker who preferred to spend his evenings in the local bars with cronies rather than working hard to advance himself intellectually or financially. Mr. R. was born in the second year of this marriage, and by the time his sister was born, he felt he was superior to his father, was destined for great things, was charming and brilliant, and was much like the revered, dead grandfather—or would soon become so. Unlike his father, he could already appreciate and understand poetry, novels, and political and economic problems which he heard about on the radio, from his mother's readings to him, and in discussions with adults. His sister's birth, he thought, had led to only a minor and transient deflation. He continued to feel preferred and superior and treated her with contempt and condescension, as he thought his mother did.

When he was sent to a local school under religious auspices at age six, he suffered a great blow. Though he thought he was more intelligent than the other children, academically more gifted and generally superior, he was disliked and excluded by them, felt physically large and inept, and was unable to make friends. He had to make do with being a teacher's pet. Throughout his childhood and adolescence, he felt deprived, lonely, and angry because he seemed unable to make friends and felt he was not one of the group. Partly, these feelings were the result of his view of himself as special and imaginative, but unappreciated. He described his behavior at this time as ingratiating and passive with peers, sparkling and brilliant with adults—for example, with teachers with whom he discussed subtle theological points. He was extremely fearful, avoided fights and arguments, and could not stand up for himself. He was a "sissy" and a "mama's boy." However, he did well enough academically to be transferred to a special school for gifted children and later to win a scholarship to a prestigious university. Nevertheless, in adolescence, as in childhood, he lacked self-confidence. He could not approach girls, came to feel he was under the thumb of his mother and the clergy, and began to resent his father for his lack of involvement with him, as well as for the other flaws that he and his mother agreed his father had. He resented the college he attended because he felt it was too strict and too much his mother's choice, but he could not bring himself to transfer. Instead, he cut classes, stayed out at night later than the rules allowed, and was almost expelled. This experience frightened and cowed him. He attended graduate school in New York, lived with his parents, and continued to bask in his mother's approval—which was withdrawn when he showed signs of independent interest, especially in women. He did not move out of his parents' home until he reached his mid-thirties.

At this time he began to form a more affectionate and understanding relation with his father and to conceive a new view of his mother. Gradually, he came to regard her as manipulative and exploitative and a millstone around his neck. When he moved out of the convenient and comfortable parental home into his own apartment, he began to date more seriously, met his wife to be, and married.

Having given something of an overview of the manner of Mr. R.'s presentation and of his history, I will now proceed to a description of the course of his analysis. Mr. R. was a tall man, six feet three inches in height, but not of impressive appearance. His frame was not broad, his appearance pudgy and soft, and he was perhaps thirty pounds overweight. He was very involved with his dress and owned many clothes, including some dozens of suits. He favored large patterns in expensive and conservative materials but in odd, bright colors. His manner matched his appearance. It was correct, yet incorrect, acquiescent, yet assertive. He would come into the office, lie down on the couch, and speak in a professorial, somewhat arrogant, lecturing manner. For several weeks he spoke in meticulous detail of his history, as though he were reciting a book. He seemed hardly to pay any attention to me, except for polite hellos or goodbyes. There was little hint of the state of his feelings or of more than a scholarly interest in the story he was unfolding.

In the second month I began to make comments to Mr. R. to the effect that there was something official in his manner, that he revealed few feelings, that he seemed to concentrate on historical matters. He was annoyed and responded by telling me that he had thought psychoanalysts were particularly interested in the histories of their patients and that he would be pleased to discuss whatever I might think best. He wished to cooperate as best he could. Perhaps he should talk more about current problems. And so he began to tell me about the office politics and the difficulties of the projects he was working on. Gradually, I told him he wished to think of me as a guide or as a "Guru," as the boss who had hired him was, someone to please and satisfy in the hope of being led. He agreed with me, noting that he was aware that I was an expert in my field, that he had come to me for help, that he hoped I would be able to explain his problems to him. Again, gradually, repeatedly, I pointed out that he seemed to act as though his observations or ideas about himself were of little account, that he wanted to leave most of the thinking about him to me, and that this seemed inconsistent with the common aim we both had to understand him and his difficulties in being more active. It also seemed inconsistent with his attitude of intellectual superiority.

Slowly, the work became somewhat more spontaneous and immediate. Mr. R. expressed some angry feelings about his years of religious indoctrination. He complained about the narrowness of his mother's and his teachers' views and concluded that his inhibitions had resulted from his "brainwashing" upbringing. He rarely spoke of his own impulses, wishes, or intentions, or indicated that he had any, other than to satisfy the desires of his employer, wife, analyst, and others, and he felt guilty and resentful about being imperfectly able to do so. I was able to convey to him that he had nevertheless told me of his opinions and attitudes about business, of disagreements with others throughout his life, of feelings of disdain for colleagues and superiors, of fears of fighting and of punishment.

Again, over a period of time, and with numerous such interchanges, Mr. R.'s manner gradually changed. He spoke of his anger with his mother and his feelings of ineptness and inadequacy. He never could live up to her expectations and thus felt incompetent or helpless in many instances. He revealed that he masturbated frequently and compulsively even now, two or three times a day, and that he had done so since adolescence. Later, with much shame, he described fantasies of being shown how to do it by an older man, then of arousing himself by fantasies of watching two women arousing each other orally, then having intercourse with dildos. I pointed out to him his tendency to make himself aloof, distant, an observer, even in his fantasies. Fears of losing control began to come up. Mr. R. remembered having frightening dreams in childhood—dreams of gory automobile crashes related to fear of his drunken father, dreams of robbers and murderers against whom he had to defend his family, especially his mother and sister. I suggested to Mr. R. that in the preceding period of his analysis, he seemed to have behaved toward me as he described his behavior toward adults in his early childhood. That is, he adopted a seemingly ingratiating manner, acting like a "goody-goody," a compliant student. Probably he hid his feelings of rivalry and contempt for the feared rival. His attitude toward superiors at work appeared to parallel his behavior toward me. His repeated infatuation with bosses and jobs, followed invariably by feelings of disappointment and disillusionment, reflected, besides fear over rivalrous wishes, an emulation of his mother's attitude of disappointment with his father and superiority to him, thus revealing his close tie to his mother.

Gradually, the patient became more querulous with me. He responded more and more to my comments with associations that took the form of "yes, but." At the same time he more frequently felt anger toward his work superiors and even openly questioned and opposed them. Rare dreams, dimly remembered, concerned battles and revolutions. His potency problem became worse. He became overtly angry with his mother, refused to see her over long periods of time or even to speak with her on the telephone. He recalled adolescent feelings of resentment toward women in general. Mr. R. came to see his rebellion against religion during his teens, his unproductivity at work, and his sexual negativism toward his wife as expressions and defenses against his underlying hostility toward his mother, whom he wished to torture by depriving her of the satisfaction of her wish to dominate him while living vicariously through him. He also thought he had "seen through" the members of the clergy who deluded themselves, thinking they were pious, when actually they craved power and domination. His method for concealing arrogance derived from identification with clergy rivals as well as with mother. Mr. R. came to understand that he had a belief that he was dependent on his mother, later on his father, teachers, the "Gurus," on his wife and on the analyst, and that criticisms by them led to the fear of being "lost," unable to fend for himself, and to feelings of extreme anger. He talked about how angry he felt when interpretations indicated that he could not "orient" himself; he then felt like withdrawing and withholding. His submissive attitude and his passive posture toward superiors diminished. He quit his job and began to search for a better position.

During this period of career transition, Mr. R. felt an uncomfortable, variable anxiety, which he blamed on me. I had deprived him of his hope that he would achieve success by attaching himself to a powerful male. I had frustrated him in his wishes to outdo his mother at her own game, to succeed where she had failed. I had caused his potency symptom to worsen. I had pointed out to him his envy of his sister, who had married a wealthy and successful businessman and had thus succeeded where he could not. I was able to expand on earlier interpretations. I explained these angry feelings as reflecting resentment at the messenger who told unwelcome truths. We were able to enlarge Mr. R.'s understanding of his adoption of a feminine attitude in terms of earlier relations within his family, as well as to clarify his fears about his competitive and hostile strivings, especially in relation to feelings of guilt over his superiority. The sexual disturbance continued. Mr. R.'s anxiety and anger focused more on his wife's wish to have a child. He would then be replaced as a favorite by the child as he had been with his father when his sister was born. He would become a "meal ticket" as his father had been. I remained puzzled about the reason for the intensity of his need to conceal his ambitiousness, the intensity of his feelings of vulnerability, the intensity of his anxiety.

In the fourth year of analysis symptomatic acts he had earlier experienced in other contexts now appeared in relation to me. He arrived late for our appointments, neglected my bills, and misremembered what had been said in preceding sessions.

117

Investigation of his mental lapses proceeded in response to my requests for further details, requests which were influenced by my puzzlement about the intensity of the feelings of mortification and humiliation Mr. R. had when parapraxes occurred. He was unable to give any reasons why he felt so humiliated over his "mistakes" or so reluctant to investigate them. His parapraxes seemed motivated in part by transference fear of me. He wished to appear a harmless, incompetent, childish person. The reasons for the intense anxiety remained obscure. I now became more curious about the form the parapraxes took.

A pattern became evident over a period of months. Mr. R. misfiled my bills. On describing the geography of his home office, he said he had put my bill in the file on the left, not in the appropriate one on the right. After a lateness, he explained that he had turned in the wrong direction in the subway and gotten on a train leading away from my office. The following night he reported remembering a dream. In it, he was interviewing an applicant for a job (he had just recently found one for himself) and rejected him. When he awoke, it was some time before he realized this had been a dream, not a reality. In the interim, he wondered whether he had been "right" in rejecting the applicant. In the session, he suggested that his sense of humiliation with me had to do with the feeling that "I am never right. I want to reverse our relationship and be right." On another occasion, as he was discussing a political office problem in which he was arguing a point with the head of his company, he explained that the "head" had been on his right, and he gestured with his left hand. I pointed out a transference connection I thought was related—Mr. R. had recently seen me driving and envied me my car—as a partial explanation of his underlying anxiety: perhaps he wished to be the "head." Was the gesture with the left hand a gesture toward the driver's seat? He had gestured with his left hand while describing the "head" who sat on his right. I was also dimly aware that the emphasis on geography—location—might have some significance.

Mr. R. responded with much embarrassment. Again he had made a slip. He felt humiliated, incompetent, like a child. He could not tell right from left. I suggested that the right-left question might be important. I pointed out the spatial confusion in the episodes of the misfiled bills, his taking the wrong direction, the dream question, "who was right?" Mr. R. became angry; I wanted to make him feel small. I had no "right" to suggest that he had a defect. I had not made this suggestion, I replied. Why did he think he had become so angry? He replied that I was mocking him for his left-handedness. His father had mocked him when he had difficulty learning to write. That he was left-handed was news to me, I indicated, as was the fact that he had had difficulty learning to write. It had never occurred to him to mention these two facts, he said. He recalled a painful memory, from the age of about four, of having gone shopping with his mother and having lost her. He had been terrified about being lost, unable to find his way to her.

This new element in the patient's life was explored and defined and its ramifications revealed to some degree. Again, feelings of guilt and fear consequent to his wish to defeat his father, and me, played a part in motivating his inhibitions. In addition, his anxiety was related to his fear that criticism indicated to him that he could not find his own way, lacked an independent ability to orient himself, and had to depend on others. He was a "faker" because he pretended that he did not have to depend on others. His writing problem and his difficulty in orienting himself in childhood had been the source of deeply humiliating feelings to him and had aggravated his anger when he felt neglected by those on whom he depended. He had also had great difficulty in spelling correctly as a child. He had never learned to spell letter by letter as other children did, but had overcome this problem by memorizing how words looked. This was a secret he had never told, because it indicated to him that he had a defect that he had to conceal to avoid being laughed at, and it contributed to his idea that he was a "faker" who concealed an embarrassing flaw.

A certain characteristic lack of humor, particularly about himself, came to seem connected to his early responses to and persisting tendency toward spatial confusion. He felt he had a defect. Something was missing that others had. Mr. R. soon thought that this "defect" played a part in his feminine identification. He had equated his spatial problem with a lack of masculinity. His physical clumsiness added to his sense of inadequate masculinity and to his sense of dependence and enforced passivity. Childhood fears and memories of being lost continued to come up, as did the relation of these experiences to later interests and characteristics. He had early become extremely interested in travel and maps. He had developed his visual capacity, his preferred visual imagery, and had come to emphasize sexual looking, as, for example, in his peeping masturbatory fantasies. He recalled a persisting difficulty in remembering which was the "x" and which was the "y" axis in high school math. His interest in organizing companies, in ordering administrative structures, in market identification, in futurology, came to seem related partly (there were various determinants) to a need to locate himself spatially, to know where he was in relation to others. His clumsiness in childhood was more closely described, and Mr. R. theorized that his tendency "to find the banana peel in life and slip on it," and the mirth it provoked in others, had added to his angry, defensive negativism, his fear of competition, and his lack of humor and spontaneity. After all, he believed he had a "defect." The banana peel image was unusual for Mr. R., who, as noted, had rarely permitted himself to be comical.

Another aspect of his childhood cognitive difficulty emerged through further memories Mr. R. recovered, relating to how he learned to read in the second and third grades, with the help of a special personage in his life, a teacher who took a special interest in him. As noted, he could not manage the abstraction of letters signifying sounds, but instead learned how words look and how to reproduce their appearance. In a way he felt a cheat, an impostor who pretended to read and write but could not really do so. He was afraid of being found out and felt guilty about being a pretender. Clearly, this "defect," so strenuously denied, concealed, and compensated for, also served as a defense against phallic aggressive strivings. The defect also made the satisfaction of these strivings seem unlikely to the patient. At the same time, his capacity to visualize supported his sense of being special and superior. He used his defect as a defense—it helped him to appear innocuous—and he defended himself against his profound feelings of defectiveness by emphasizing his superior qualities. At the same time, his pride over his capacity to visualize contributed to his anxious fantasies about impending punishment.

In his new capacity for greater ambition and aggressiveness Mr. R. now determined to have a child but discovered he was sterile. He attempted various medical treatments to remedy his new defect but was unsuccessful. Six months later, he arranged to adopt a baby, was pleased with good success at his new job, and had only a moderate fear mixed with his enjoyment of the political wars at work. Sexual ennui persisted and so did his masturbatory fantasies. He was able to recognize and understand feelings of anger and depression related to the recent blow of discovering his sterility, but claimed adoption would be a satisfactory solution. At this point, he said he was satisfied with the analytic results and was determined to end his treatment. As reasons for a more abrupt termination than I would have regarded as optimal, he cited questions of time and money related to job and child, and an unwillingness to enter into a struggle with his insurance company, which was demanding lengthy reports on his condition.

The insurance question was unfortunate, but significant, because it played into his continuing anxiety about his defects and his persisting tendency to defend against feelings of anxiety and depression related to them. It also influenced his decision to take his life "into his own hands" at this time.

I have presented a case report of the treatment of a middle-aged man who came to treatment because of work problems and sexual dysfunction. In the course of the analysis, we came upon what seemed to be hints of a cognitive difficulty. Memories appeared that confirmed the presence of difficulties and of special childhood abilities that had contributed to his problems in adult life and to his character development. In childhood, this left-handed patient had suffered from right-left confusion, impulsiveness, lexical problems respecting the written word, clumsiness, and some difficulty involving abstraction, or perhaps the capacity to categorize the significant and less significant. He also thought he had a special ability to visualize and to remember. In adulthood, he was inhibited, controlled, passive, humorless, fearful about competing, passively aggressive, and sexually dysfunctional. He was also methodical, rigorous, interested in structure, visually gifted, and felt guiltily and fearfully superior. The treatment had clear, positive, but limited results. Mr. R. became more successful at work and in his relationships. He will probably enjoy fatherhood, but he remained relatively constricted and somewhat anxious. He learned a great deal but was unable to work analytically in a termination phase. His departure seemed to reflect a newfound ability to be more active, but it also seemed to suppress his only partly analyzed aggression and his transference fears of punishment, now in relation to fantasies about fatherhood. Certain characteristics were relatively unaffected by the analysis. His responsiveness to interventions in general remained less spontaneous and original than that of many other patients. His dream reports remained rare, and his associations unimaginative, perhaps vaguely concrete. At the same time, he maintained an arrogant sense of superiority which compensated him to some extent for his continuing feelings of defectiveness, but his guilt and fear of retaliation, which he was able to analyze to some degree, persisted and contributed to his decision to terminate.

I return to the original Question 1 about how one can detect previously unrecognized cognitive difficulties in analysis. In this case, a number of the patient's adult characteristics led to my suspicion that such difficulties might have been present in childhood. These included certain characterologic qualities. They were general qualities: an underlying level of anxiety and a corresponding defensiveness, a narcissistic vulnerability and rigidity of character, a distance and humorlessness, and a constriction of dream and fantasy life that seemed out of keeping, in my clinical judgment, with the historic factors that I knew and with his general competence. The severity of Mr. R.'s separation problems and the intensity of his bisexual conflicts were more specific factors that led me to wonder. Still more specific keys involved his propensity to feel humiliation, almost mortification, in response to seemingly minor parapraxes and, finally, his repeated use of imagery involving location, particularly in relation to right and left in his associations, as well as in many parapraxes. Ultimately, these cues led to the discovery of Mr. R.'s childhood lexical difficulties, writing problems, clumsiness, and spatial uncertainties. This grouping corresponds to Wender's (1971) description of minimal brain dysfunction: Mr. R. had "impaired coordination," "clumsiness," "problems in arithmetic" (including the x-y axis confusion), "short attention span" (which seemed to persist and to influence Mr. R.'s work performance), "impulsivity," and an "obsessive quality."

As to Questions 2 and 3 regarding the effect of these difficulties on development and on the patient as analysand, the effects—e.g., heightened anxiety and defensiveness, and their developmental vicissitudes—became obvious during the course of the work. Mr. R.'s sense of defect had supported his vulnerability to separation at first and his susceptibility to castration fears later. The sense of defect added to his sense of loss at his sister's birth, and later, when he went to school, it contributed to his tendency toward depressive ideas of incompetence and dependence, to his susceptibility to ridicule, to his humorlessness, and to his tendency toward sulking and withholding. It also spurred him to compensatory development of his visual capacities and to efforts at finding alternative ways of orienting himself spatially and temporally.

Regarding Question 4, about the possibility of needing to modify technique with such patients, I do not believe that this case required technical modification, although it was necessary to repeat interpretations in various words, using a variety of examples, more patiently and tactfully than usual. This seems to be similar to tutorial methods used to aid children with cognitive difficulties, which depend on presenting concepts in alternate forms and using a variety of sensory modalities to aid the child in finding alternative routes around his difficulties. It might be that in a more seriously impaired patient than Mr. R. was, more literal and concrete examples and analogies would have to be given, to convey the meaning intended in an intervention. In some instances, a supportive, encouraging, more psychotherapeutic approach may be required.

As to Question 5, having to do with the issue of etiology, I do not personally think that psychoanalytic data can be used as definitive evidence regarding the question of immanent versus developmental factors. In Mr. R.'s case there is perhaps a piece of negative evidence: none of his cognitive idiosyncrasies could be explained to my satisfaction, in the way that symptoms, dreams, and other psychological phenomena can, simply as the consequence of compromise formation. Nor did his tendency toward right-left confusion or his difficulty in organizing his ideas and in sometimes translating images into words significantly change with analysis. It is possible that Mr. R.'s functioning deteriorated more readily under stress than one might expect on dynamic and developmental grounds. Perhaps, under stress, characteristic forms appeared because of an underlying physiological organization which became mobilized for psychologic reasons. It is clear that Mr. R. used the forms for defensive and wish-gratifying aims, both consciously and automatically.

Finally, I would like to speculate briefly about why this subject has received little attention from psychoanalysts. First, until recent years, it has received little attention from anyone. The likelihood is that had Mr. R. had his reading difficulty as a child today, a diagnosis of dyslexia would have been made, and remedial efforts would have been instituted. He might have been referred for psychotherapy or analysis as well. Second, such difficulties have received attention in recent years, but mainly as a problem of children, not as a problem of adults. It must occur often that such difficulties in childhood have, as they did for Mr. R., important effects on the development of later pathologic and characterologic formations, just as physical infirmities, illnesses, or such defects as color blindness do. That they may persist and continue to affect cognition may also be so. But this has not been generally recognized. Thus if the difficulty is subtle, it may not be recognized. If severe, such patients may not be considered candidates for analysis.

REFERENCES

Rosen, V.H. (1955). Strephosymbolia: An intrasystemic disturbance of the synthetic function of the ego *Psychoanal. Study Child* 10:83–99.

——— (1961). The relevance of 'style' to certain aspects of defence and the synthetic function of the ego *Int. J. Psychoanal.* 42:447–457.

Weil, A. P. (1978). Maturational variations and genetic-dynamic issues *J. Am. Psychoanal. Assoc.* 26:461–491.

Wender, P.H. (1971). *Minimal Brain Dysfunction in Children*. New York: Wiley & Sons.

CHAPTER 7

On Examination Dreams

(1979). *Psychoanalytic Quarterly*, 48:426–447

ABSTRACT

The literature concerning examination dreams is reviewed, and the case of a patient who had a number of examination and examination-like dreams is described. Examination dreams are related to traumatic dreams, "idiosyncratic" dreams, and various behavioral expressions. In addition, constitutional factors involving impulse-defense imbalance, childhood experiences with physical difficulties and medical examinations, and ambivalent identifications and object relations seem to find representation in these dreams.

In his first analytic hour, a twenty-four-year-old male patient related an anxiety dream that closely resembled those described by Freud in 1900 as "typical" examination dreams. During the course of the analysis, the young man described having had similar dreams many times prior to the analysis. He reported several other such dreams during the early years of his analysis. The analysis revealed much about the sources, functions, vicissitudes, and relationships of the dreams to other aspects of the patient's mental life.

The prominence of examination dreams in this analysis suggested that reviewing the case and the literature on examination dreams might lead to some ideas and conclusions about the role of this kind of dream organization that might have been insufficiently emphasized in the past.

The conclusion was reached that important aspects of the patient's examination dreams could be understood in ways that previous authors had outlined: (1) that they were related to other anxiety dreams and "traumatic" dreams as well as to characterological behavioral expressions; (2) that they served as a form of reassurance in the face of anticipated danger; and (3) that they represented a modified form of a "traumatic" dream growing out of transference responses in which early experiences of helplessness were activated.

There seemed, however, to be additional important factors, insufficiently emphasized in the literature, that determined the organization of the dream: (1) constitutional factors involving impulse-defense imbalance may have played an etiological role; (2) childhood physical problems, which subjected the patient to painful experiences with doctors, were significant; and (3) ambivalent oedipal and preoedipal conflicts and identifications played an important part in the choice of the figures who entered the dreams.

Another point of interest is that during this patient's analysis, changes took place in the examination dreams. They paralleled his increasing freedom and spontaneity and his decreasing "typicalness" in other respects.

Finally, it seemed worthwhile to emphasize the importance of the role of representability in understanding both the typicality and the repetitiveness of these dreams.

REVIEW OF THE LITERATURE

The psychoanalytic understanding of examination dreams began when Freud (1900) called attention to them as "typical" dreams. As with other mental phenomena, our understanding of them continued to evolve as later authors added new insights, modifications, and elaborations to augment Freud's original explanations.

In *The Interpretation of Dreams,* Freud (1900) distinguished «a certain number of dreams which almost everyone has dreamt alike... which we... assume must have the same meaning for everyone... [and which] presumably arise from the same sources in every case,» as opposed to those which reflect the dreamer›s «individual peculiarities.» Such «typical dreams» frustrate their would-be interpreter because characteristically «the dreamer fails... to produce the associations which would in other cases have led us to understand [them]" (p. 241).

Among the typical dreams, Freud included anxiety dreams with the manifest content of having failed an examination. The subject awakens with a feeling of relief: "It was only a dream actually, since I've already passed." Freud said: "In the case of those who have obtained a University degree, this typical dream is replaced by another one which represents them as having failed in their University Finals; and it is in vain that they object, even while they are still asleep, that for years they have been practising medicine or working as University lecturers or heads of offices" (pp. 273–274). Such dreams, according to Freud, "appear when the dreamer has some responsible activity ahead of him... and is afraid there may be a fiasco," a situation that revives memories of punishment for evil deeds of childhood (p. 274). The parent as a feared figure is replaced by a schoolmaster and then by an examination. Since the subject of the examination in the dream is one which the dreamer has already passed, the dream serves as a "consolation... 'Don't be afraid of tomorrow!... You're a doctor, etc., already'" (p. 274). Freud thus pointed to a reassurance aspect, which has been confirmed by other investigators.

An element of guilty self-criticism stemming from a feeling of having slipped through the examination that had been passed via collusion with the examiner was, according to Freud, another latent content. The latent self-criticism takes the form: "You're quite old…" to still be doing "stupid, childish things," which refers to "sexual acts" (pp. 275–276). Without specifically stating it, Freud thus alluded to a self-disciplinary, impulse-controlling wish as a latent content.

Sadger (1920) described a patient with examination anxiety and also a dream in which he was unable to answer a school examiner's question. Sadger concluded that the patient's dream had been stimulated by sexual excitement and by current sexual success. The anxiety both in the dream and in the examination situations was castration anxiety. Sadger's patient had unconscious-guilt over an unconscious fantasy of having intercourse with his mother and stealing her from his father, stimulated by the observation of coitus between his parents. The patient's low self-esteem effected childhood feelings of inferiority related to ignorance of how coitus is performed. The unknown was the mother's genital which in childhood he did not know in fact, but which he did know, guiltily, in fantasy. The dream was an effort to deny the fantasy and expiate the guilt. In a subsequent examination dream, the manifest content was of obtaining a solution to a problem from a friend, but too late to use it. Sadger's understanding of the patient was largely on the level of oedipal conflict. He also alluded to an equivalence between the dream and a symptomatic formation of waking life, examination anxiety, and expanded our understanding of examination dreams by including the dream in which a friend assisted the dreamer in that category.

In terms similar to those that Sadger had applied to the examination dream, Blum (1926) wrote of a woman with examination anxiety, but without examination dreams: he concluded that examination anxiety reflects oedipal guilt. Blum implied that the symptom and the dream are parallel. He also thought that he found contributions from preoedipal conflicts, however. Guilt and fear of punishment, consisting in loss of the mother, he felt, leads to prohibition against passing the examination. Blum compared the examination situation with the initiation rites of primitive peoples. He suggested that dream, symptom, and rite have similar purposes. He felt that they have to do with conflicts of the oedipal period and that they reflect regression from intense oedipal conflict, enhanced by unresolved preoedipal conflicts. Apparently, initiation rites have the social function of helping the individual master developmental difficulties.

Schmideberg (1933) described a patient who had had a "typical" examination dream. Her patient, in a dream, had been unable to remember a word during an examination. She understood the patient's examination dream, his examination anxiety, and his transferential difficulty in associating in analysis as the consequence of a fear that the examiner would take away his penis and power, which he himself had stolen in a sadistic, unconscious fantasy. She described the analyst as a figure who enters into the examination dream as a new representative of the feared castrator.

Stengel (1936) expanded our understanding of examination anxiety by connecting it with neurotic fears about performance, potency disturbances, fate neuroses, and perverse masochism, which he attributed to reactivated oedipal conflicts and pubertal intergenerational rivalry. Those who see life as a test, he stated, do so because of the persistent need to establish a feeling of mastery. The unresolved conflicts may manifest themselves in neurotic attitudes toward examination in which the examiner is viewed either as overly strict or as lenient, reflecting an etiologic overstrictness or leniency of the father.

Stengel concluded that patients with examination anxiety have an unusual need to establish a sense of mastery, that examination dreams are related to a variety of inhibitions, and that subjects partly resolve their underlying conflicts by identifying with examiners. He described the problem of examination fear not only in terms of sources and meanings, but also in terms of a possible evolution into an identification with the object of rivalry. He thereby suggested that the examination problem occupies a place in developmental evolution.

Flügel (1939) suggested that examination anxiety has a function similar to that of primitive rites, in that both deal with overdetermined castration anxiety. Rites, he stated, symbolically carry out the castration only to restore the penis subsequently, facilitating identification with the castrator. He did not, however, clearly explain the relationship between examination anxiety and the partial resolution of castration anxiety by means of rites carried out by helping figures who participate in them.

From Freud, Sadger, Blum, Schmideberg, Stengel, and Flügel, we have come to see examination dreams as regressive phenomena reflecting conflict between oedipal wishes, guilts, and fears, presumably with contributions from conflicts stemming from earlier developmental periods. The issues involved in the dreams can also be expressed symptomatically as examination and performance anxiety in primitive rites of passage and in transference responses in analytic treatment. In the rites and in treatment, the "examiner" plays a useful role in helping the developing individual master his or her anxieties.

Bonaparte (1947) went beyond the theories that explained the examination dream solely in terms of internal conflict when she suggested that examination dreams may be the successors of traumatic dreams. She reported a case of a lion hunter who had almost been killed by a lion, but had been able to save himself and kill the beast. Years later, he had repeated dreams of being unable to kill attacking lions; each time he would awake on the point of being killed. The manifest performance inhibition presumably related these dreams to examination dreams. Bonaparte proposed that, because the hunter had actively saved himself, he had recovered sufficiently for his dreams to go beyond a monotonous replication of the traumatic event. They had evolved instead into a type of examination dream (although an examination in the strict sense was not a direct part of the manifest content). He could not remember the dreams he had had shortly after having been mauled. Bonaparte speculated that they may have been true traumatic dreams. Bonaparte's main contribution was the idea that traumatization can be a factor preceding the construction of examination dreams.

Kanzer (1949) reported a case of a soldier with nightmares of being pursued by a Japanese soldier and unable to respond. This "traumatic dream" replicated a real event. Although associations in a strict sense were unavailable, in a wider sense they were. In an amytal interview, the soldier revealed that there was an underlying crime for which the dream served as punishment: on several occasions he had killed enemy troops himself. Early death wishes against a rival, an older brother, became apparent. To Kanzer, these partly explained the intensity of the guilt. The nightmares gradually became less anxious and stereotyped, because, said Kanzer, with the help of the forgiving therapist, unconscious mourning rituals, akin to the customs of savages who seek to appease their victims, were carried out by the patient. Kanzer thus supported Bonaparte's idea. He demonstrated the relationship between a stereotyped, repeated traumatic dream and its traumatic precursors in waking life and in a pre-existing psychic conflict. He showed that such dreams can change, losing their typicality, with therapeutic success. In Kanzer's case, the therapist seems to have played a role somewhat like that of the helper in a primitive rite.

Ward (1961) also regarded examination dreams as existing in a continuum that starts with trauma and traumatic dreams. He felt that in examination dreams, the ego attempts to deal with persistent, recurrent, traumatogenic behavior patterns involving "passive aggressive defiance, covert seduction or frank deception of authority, or inappropriate self-aggrandizement," through "an integrative effort in the specific sense of lessening guilt" (p. 335). Ward's observations supported those of Kanzer in indicating that the patient can use the therapist to help him modify his self-punitive tendencies. As aggression diminishes, Ward implied, the patient converts the examiner into a helper. He also provided further evidence to support the idea of the additive influences of traumatic experiences and intrapsychic conflict.

McLaughlin (1961) reported on a case of a physician who, in a situation of heightened intellectual competitiveness with the analyst following a success in a field of mutual interest, dreamed that he was being examined by a physician on the subject of the anatomy of the eye. In the dream, he was able to answer only incompletely, and he failed. McLaughlin interpreted the dream as reflecting the patient's need to adopt a submissive role. The patient equated intellectual ambitions with covert oedipal ones and resolved the issue through guilty submission via identification with his sick mother "whose illness won her gratifying associations with physicians" (p. 121). McLaughlin emphasized the consolation or reassurance implied in submission to the physician and ultimately to the mother, related to the necessity of replacing a needed but lost (through illness) nurturing parent. He thus further underlined the interrelation between traumatic events (in this case, illness of the mother) and intrapsychic conflicts in the determination of an examination dream. He added the observation that his patient's dream also incorporated an early identification with his mother.

Arlow (1959), in discussing *déjà vu*, quoted Freud on the examination dream, which Arlow regarded as a related phenomenon carrying the message, «Don›t worry, don›t be afraid, no harm will come to you this time either» (p. 627). Arlow added that to the extent that the consolation is unsuccessful, a «lingering sense of uneasiness, of the uncanny» persists (in the *déjà vu*), indicating that the ego has not succeeded in "mastering" the "underlying anxiety." This gives impetus to the idea of placing the examination dream in a continuum in which the dream reflects an attempt to master a pre-existing anxiety.

The various contributions reviewed above provide us with the following understanding of examination dreams. These dreams are similar to various normal behaviors (for example, rites of passage), symptomatic expressions (such as *déjà vu* and examination anxiety), and transference responses (such as inhibition of free association), as well as to traumatic dreams and anxiety dreams. These phenomena are similar formally (a powerful, observing person in relationship with a weak acolyte type), phenomenologically (the subject experiences anxiety, a sense of incapacity to execute an intention, and heightened self-consciousness), and functionally (to provide reassurance and enhance power by the subject›s becoming more like the powerful figure). Obviously, these phenomena also differ from one another.

Bonaparte and Ward suggested that a traumatic dream precedes the later appearance of an examination dream. The latter can be thought of as reflecting a certain degree of recovery from traumatization. All authors agree that the examination dream serves the same defensive and wish-fulfilling functions reflecting intrapsychic conflict states that other dreams do. It is stimulated by day residues that stimulate unresolved wishes or threaten defenses. It contains interpretable, latent contents related to conflicts organized at differing levels of development.

CASE REPORT

Mr. A was twenty-four years old when he consulted a colleague because of the feeling that his life was unsatisfying and not purposeful or under his control. He feared that he lacked a capacity to be interested in work or to feel affection for people, especially for women. He thought of himself as a drifter, an outsider, a "Flying Dutchman," not involved in life. Two factors had led him to seek advice. One was that a two-year relationship with a woman had ended because he had been unable to satisfy her wishes for marriage or at least for greater emotional response. The second was that he had been passed over for promotion. These events had caused an intensification of long-standing feelings of self-doubt, uncertainty, inferiority, and depression. The consultant told Mr. A that he suffered from a chronic depression and advised him to undergo analysis.

In his initial interviews with me, Mr. A seemed somewhat listless and depressed. He gave the following personal history. Because of family financial reverses Mr. A's father had to give up his ambition for a professional career. While in his mid-thirties, Mr. A's father married a woman fifteen years his junior. A year later, Mr. A was born. The family's financial circumstances were straitened. All three members shared a single bedroom. Mr. A's father worked at two jobs and therefore had relatively little contact with the patient. Mr. A and his mother, on the other hand, were very close. She was said to have doted on him; he was "the apple of her eye." When the patient was five, his mother gave birth to a second son, and, their financial circumstances having improved, the family moved to larger quarters where Mr. A had his own room. He was enrolled in school (kindergarten), his first departure from home. The patient had apparently developed a moderate depression at this time. He felt lost and deprived and began to get along badly with his father, who seemed critical toward and

136

resentful of him. Rivalry over intellectual prowess was to remain a lifelong, central issue in Mr. A's relationship with his father. Mr. A adapted poorly in school. Initially, he was fearful, clumsy, bumped into things, and had difficulty learning to read. After the first years he developed rapidly intellectually, but did not develop good relationships with his peers. He was a mama's boy, unathletic and timorous about physical activity, and was teased by his classmates. When he was six or seven years old, his mother developed an illness that was later diagnosed as a mild form of lupus. This entailed visits to doctors, trips to hospitals, and a varying but continual amount of cranky self-centeredness on her part. Mr. A remembered little of his early relationship with his brother, but described having adopted a maternal, affection-ate attitude toward him in latency and thereafter.

Mr. A said that he gradually became more independent. He developed friendships with other young men in high school and college, but was not able to overcome significant anxiety with women until he had graduated from college. Then he began to have sexual relations with "liberated" women who made the initial advances. At twenty-five, Mr. A joined a large firm where he settled into his current, middle-level administrative job.

In his first analytic hour, Mr. A described some discomfort at being on the couch because he could not see my expression and thereby know whether he was relating "interesting material." He had some doubts about whether he would be able to succeed as an analysand. He said that he was due to make a presentation to his supervisor that day, but did not feel that he had prepared adequately. He wondered whether I would be satisfied with his performance. He now related a dream which he introduced as one of his "typical" dreams about not being prepared or not knowing the answer.

Dream 1

"I dreamed about this last night, only it wasn't about you. It was about my boss. I was afraid. I arrived late for today's presentation, and then I couldn't answer. When I woke up I realized it had just been a dream and I'd probably do okay on the presentation."

Mr. A went on to note that on the preceding day, he had failed to proofread some material that he had circulated before his presentation. The supervisor had pointed out some errors to him, in an uncritical way. Mr. A had felt guilty because, instead of correcting his copy, he had gone to the movies. In subsequent hours that week, he spoke of latency period feelings of being excluded by his critical, distant father and of loneliness after the birth of his brother.

Mr. A was told that his wish to please the analyst was similar to his wish to please his parents and his boss. He responded by recalling angry feelings toward his brother at the time of the brother's birth and later on. He was told that his submissive, ingratiating attitude was intended to conceal rivalrous and hostile feelings, which he had covertly expressed by inadequately preparing his work for the boss and by filling a good bit of analytic time with reports of worries that he might not please the analyst. His main wish at this point was to feel reassured that, as with the dream boss, he would continue to have someone with him, someone with questions, perhaps, but someone present.

This first dream reflected some of Mr. A's characteristic anxieties and his mechanisms for dealing with them. The lateness and the incapacity to respond in the dream paralleled his worrying during the analytic sessions and his failure to complete his work and reflected a certain negativism rooted in his rivalry with his brother and father.

The passive, ingratiating, and somewhat masochistic attitudes he expressed in relation to his boss and his analyst and, earlier, in relation to his parents, served to expiate guilt over hostile feelings, to avoid punishment for them, and to assure himself of the ongoing presence of a maternally derived companion. The reassurance aspect played an important role; in the dream, in his work relationship with his supervisor, and in the analysis, he was relieved that the authority figures responded benignly, despite his provocations. Further reassurance came by way of the waking thought, "it was only a dream," which he soon described as his mother's soothing words during his childhood.

Dream 2

Anticipation of another presentation at work preceded the following dream two months later.

> "I dreamed I failed a course I needed for graduation. I knew nothing on the exam. Then I partly woke up, still half asleep, thinking, 'But I have enough credits even without this course.' Then I woke up and thought, 'But, I've graduated.'"

Mr. A remarked that he had been feeling angry with his supervisor, who had not assigned him an interesting piece of work, but had given it to another person instead. It was suggested that he might be feeling rivalrous with the other person as well as with his supervisor. Mr. A responded that his brother had just been fired from his job and had gone back to live with their mother. He was asked if he felt superior to his brother. "I guess I am, but I shouldn't feel pleased. I should help him find another job." He became hesitant at this point. He stated that he had made a date with a sexy secretary. He was worried about his ability to satisfy her. He had been quite depressed over the break-up with his previous woman friend and wondered whether his sexual performance might be affected now. Perhaps he would ejaculate prematurely. I told the patient that I thought he was suffering from guilt over wanting to outdo his brother, envy of his brother's being able to move in with their mother, and a feeling of inadequacy. Mr. A replied, "This reminds me. I may not have told you. It's probably not important. I wet the bed on and off till I was ten or eleven. Usually my mother said nothing. Several times she took me to the family doctor. He always lectured me. He said there was nothing wrong with me. I was acting like a baby. Actually, I was afraid of him. I felt humiliated and frightened." Mr. A thought that the doctor had expressed not only his own opinion but also that of Mr. A's mother—that he was an unwelcome, messy burden. The patient concurred with this view of himself.

Subsequent sessions revealed further information about Mr. A's real-life, as opposed to dream, failures. He recalled his clumsiness as a child. He used to bump into things and break them. He had had difficulty learning to ride a bicycle. His father always made fun of his unsuccessful efforts. Even the information that this very father had been enuretic until his own adolescence, which Mr. A reported that he had learned while in high school, had not made him feel better. The enuresis and clumsiness had seriously interfered with his relationships with peers, since he had constantly feared making an embarrassing slip. This fear had also evidently invaded his relationships with teachers and examiners.

The analyst's interventions at this point dealt with the patient's use of displacement of his concerns from the physical to the intellectual sphere. He had substituted a college course for the series of early childhood physical failures and inadequacies in his dream. He had used the dream examination as a screen behind which he could conceal his fear of physical inadequacy from himself and reassure himself by substituting an area in which he had generally done well. The previously repressed memories of his enuresis and clumsiness had energized, as well as been concealed in, his examination dreams. The examiner in the dream combined features of Mr. A's analyst with memories of his teachers, father, and pediatrician, while at the same time concealing them. Additionally, the information about the enuresis in father and son and about Mr. A's clumsiness suggested the possibility that defective impulse control might have contributed to the construction of the examination dream, as well as to life situations in which Mr. A submitted repeatedly to controlling disciplinarians. At times, he impulsively ate,

drank, spent money, and provoked people's anger. Doctors, teachers, and bosses were individuals whom Mr. A thought of ambivalently—as hostile to him and as potentially helpful, in that they might assist him in controlling himself.

In the analysis, discussion of Mr. A's fear of physical inadequacy, his fear of doctors, and his fear of his impulses led him to become more interested in his inability to control his weight, a problem he had hitherto avoided discussing, and he made an appointment for a physical examination.

The second dream and its attendant associations thus broadened our understanding of the patient's use of examination dreams beyond the element of reassurance against the anticipated danger of punishment for hostile, rivalrous inclinations that had become clear after the first dream. We now saw that certain constitutional and/ or developmental factors that had instilled a fear of embarrassing physical ineptitude and failure had played a role in their origin. Displacement in the examination dream to the more successful intellectual sphere provided a second form of reassurance, i.e., against narcissistic mortification.

In the dream to follow, the patient would broaden our understanding of his use of the examination dream to ward off his dread of defective functioning. He would connect it with his awareness of actual physical defects, incurred or discovered in a psychologically traumatic fashion, which unconsciously had become linked with castration anxiety stemming from positive and negative oedipal conflicts. The significance of mysterious and, hence, "unknown" defects and of physical "examinations" in the genesis of examination dreams would also become apparent.

Dream 3

The night before his physical examination, Mr. A dreamed:

> "I was having a written examination, part of a physical for the service. I knew I couldn't pass. Then there was another dream. I was boxing, trying to protect my face."

Mr. A explained that he had been rejected from military service because of a curvature of the spine. This had been on his mind the day before in anticipation of his physical examination. The boxing dream reminded him that he had had a tooth pulled a few months earlier. The dentist had informed him that he had a deviated septum. Again, the substitution of a written examination for a physical one was evident. A question to the patient about what significance the deviation of the septum and the spine might have to him, and why he had to protect himself so vigorously against them, led to recall of further memories of childhood ineptness in sports, specifically about inability to run well. He asked whether I had noticed that he walked oddly. One leg was a bit shorter than the other.

Together with an apparently lessened need to deny his defects to me, Mr. A could now consult his formerly feared childhood doctor. He learned that at age two and a half he had had an illness, presumably polio, and had been bedridden for about six weeks. He was left with a barely noticeable muscle weakness in his left leg. The defect had evidently been ignored by all concerned. I suggested that this had given the experience traumatic effect, out of proportion to the degree of actual disability and consequent frustration it had entailed. It had functioned as a piece of knowledge the patient had not been able to know consciously until his analysis. The "unknown" defect had been unconsciously regarded both as a sign of badness and as a punishment for his bad wishes toward his mother, brother, and father. Mr. A replied to the interpretation by saying that he connected the idea of deviation with homosexuality and with being a mama's boy into adult life.

His parents' silence about his illness both confirmed his feeling of being defective and stimulated his need to be cared for. It added to his castration fears, and it contributed to his later theory that his mother's illness was a consequence of the sexual activities that had led to his brother's birth as well as a punishment for them.

This third dream was interpreted as representing and negating early childhood feelings of traumatic helplessness (bed confinement, weak leg, castration) and was an effort to feel in control by enlisting the aid of a disciplinarian examiner with the right answers who could support his relatively powerless ego. The muscular defect that had been "unknown" seemed also to contribute to the dream image of "not knowing" the answers to the examination questions. The examination dreams now seemed more convincingly to have a "medical examination" component. They also appeared to serve to relieve Mr. A of responsibility for his dangerous angry feelings by projecting them onto the examiner.

Dream 4

One day, a week before a summer vacation was to interrupt the analysis, Mr. A reluctantly revealed that the day before he had made a date with a woman about whom he had lively sexual fantasies. That evening, he had to work late with his boss, with whom he felt unusually irritated. The boss was "too meticulous and critical." That night, Mr. A had a dream.

> "I had to take a test. Then I had a new job at the stock exchange, but didn't know how to read the board or work a computer I had in front of me. There was a girl at the next desk, like a high school desk, taking notes. I asked her for help but didn't understand her answer. Then in another dream, I was in elementary school with a girl who was my buddy. I was surprised, since I knew I was much older. There was a guest teacher, a doctor, and I questioned his credentials. I wanted to leave but the doctor said I had to have a shot. In the dream I thought the doctor was incompetent, not like you."

Mr. A said, "In childhood, in school, they forced us to take naps and I hated it. Yesterday I joined a health club. I'm determined to get into shape. Last night I overate. That's breaking the rules. Why bother talking about these things?" At this point, he was told, "You're guilty and fearful about your sexual wishes and think of me as though I were your childhood doctor who criticized you and caused you pain with shots. You resent me and fear me and try to make it seem that my knowing about your sexual wishes doesn't matter. You can defy us authorities." "Your interpretations make sense but don't really help," he replied. "It would be better if you gave me advice, told me how to behave." I said, "I guess your insisting I'm useless conceals something else. Maybe you're thinking about my upcoming vacation. Maybe that's a test too." At first Mr. A said that he was looking forward to the separation. He would have free time and save some money. Then he suggested that the analyst might have been the assistant whom he enlisted in his dreams. He connected a family friend with the dream assistant and brought up a memory of having been left with her shortly after the brother's birth while his parents went away with the brother. He cried each night until, finally, his parents had to return.

This dream had been stimulated by sexual excitement connected with fantasies of damage to his mother consequent to her sexual activity. Recall of his traumatic abandonment by his mother followed confrontation with his bravado about the impending interruption of the analysis. The examiner-analyst of the dream represented a wished-for nurturing mother, a repository for Mr. A's anger, and an aide in establishing self-control. The brother's birth was followed by a long, apparently depressive semi-invalidism on his mother's part, connected with her lupus. Memories appeared now of the patient's returning home from school to find his mother in bed and of spending afternoons (ages nine through twelve) amusing his brother and shopping so that his mother could sleep. His identification with his mother turned out to have various sources. One was his longing for her. Another was that both had illnesses, that both needed care which came from doctors. From this point on in the analysis, Mr. A ceased to report examination-type dreams.

The fourth and final dream, which occurred in the transferential context of impending separation from the analyst, completed our understanding of the patient's use of examination dreams to reassure himself against and ward off traumatic tension states and neurotic guilts and fears. It provided us with information about the role of preoedipal conflicts and identifications associated with the traumatic loss of his caretaking, nurturing mother consequent to the birth of a sibling and a protracted maternal illness that left him alone with his unrequited, dependent yearnings and rising drive tensions.

We came to see that the examiner in the dreams in part represented the care-giving, protecting, helping, preoedipal mother, who had partly been internalized as an element of the patient's self-representation—to be summoned up in his dreams at times of stress and fear—and was partly searched for repeatedly in the outside world. The latter took the form of seeking to establish a relationship with a protective, nurturing, reassuring, external object in the form of a helpful analyst, a forgiving and controlling boss, or a giving and loving woman friend. When this final piece of the puzzle was analytically put into place, the need for these dreams disappeared.

DISCUSSION

The following considerations seem to offer clarification of this patient's examination dreams. The dreams first appeared in the analysis in a context of apprehensive excitement regarding the patient's performance before superiors and, in the transference, before the analyst. Later he spoke extensively of underlying fears of losing a mainly maternal object. These fears were associated with clumsiness, enuresis until the age of twelve, and an illness for which he was bedridden and which left him with a weak leg and contributed to his poor sports performance. Numerous medical examinations and his mother's illness emphasized both the frightening and the maternally helpful activities of doctor-examiners. The enuresis and clumsiness suggested a possible early imbalance between impulses and capacity for self-control, although this could not be documented with certainty. (Impulsiveness was further heightened by the sexual stimulation the patient experienced while sharing his parents' bedroom.) The deviation dream led to the discovery of Mr. A's fantasies of having been castrated or warned that he might be. Fears of sexual wishes and of separation from the analyst stimulated a still later examination-like dream. At this time in the analysis, anger and sadness caused by the disruption of his close tie to his mother because of the birth of his sibling and because of her later physical illness, together with its psychological consequences, were prominent in Mr. A's thoughts and feelings. His loss of the previously close relationship with his mother, his presumed impulse control problem, and his early physical disability and its sequelae contributed to the severity of his oedipal problems and to his intense castration anxiety.

The examiner, in the various guises of boss, teacher, doctor, and parent, embodied Mr. A's self-controlling inclinations, his defensive, aggressive, and moral tendencies, and, often, his grandiose wishes. The examiner also represented helpful, appreciative, and disciplinary individuals from the past, upon whom Mr. A had relied.

The examination dreams underwent a variety of transformations and eventually disappeared. The earlier dreams were relatively sparse in manifest content and were "typical." Later dreams were more "idiosyncratic," incorporated personalities other than examiner and examinee, and were less "typical."

The reassurance first came when Mr. A was awake, then appeared in a semi-wakeful state, and then in a dream. A helper appeared in a later dream; then the doctor-examiner was denounced; and, finally, the whole examination dream construction disappeared.

In this case, the examination dream represented the psychic conflict within the patient of instinct opposed by defense by personifying these tendencies and their interrelationships in terms of historically important object relationships. Mother, father, pediatrician, aunt, and teachers at various times were prominent in the latent meaning of the relationship of examiner and examined.

147

At first, the internal struggle was portrayed as occurring at a high level of intensity: a good deal of anxiety appeared, the impulses were frightening, and their suppression was rigid. Initially, the dreams portrayed a person quite helpless in the face of the struggle. Mr. A's weak leg, the loss of his mother at the time of his brother's birth, the enuresis, his mother's illness, and his father's disparagement caused feelings of helplessness and rage that magnified his sense of weakness and his fears of loss of control and punishment, which initially had to be denied.

The examination dream also represented the helplessness which the patient had often felt, a sense of helplessness close to that following a traumatic experience. Thus the examination dream, (1) concealed helplessness, (2) represented trauma, (3) represented a mental state of intense conflict, and (4) represented developmentally important relations between Mr. A and significant objects.

The examination dream seemed particularly suitable as a vehicle for representing a number of wishful aims. (1) The intimate early relationship with the patient's mother that subsequently had been lost was retained in fantasy, via the relationship with the knowing examiner. (2) The examiner could be used to recapture the protective controlling and punishing functions of the patient's father, doctors, teachers, and other authoritarian figures from the past. (3) The dream was capable of representing the patient's dangerous impulses as having been brought under control. The need to stringently suppress impulses seemed particularly well represented by the ignorant, submissive student bending before the power of a potentially punitive examiner. The submissive aspect additionally expressed Mr. A's strong maternal identification and homosexual longings. More superficially, the patient's relationship with both parents involved ambivalences and conflicts centering about knowledge and education as the route to success.

That the examination dream could at one and the same time represent traumatic experiences of helplessness, inner psychic forces, and object relationships perhaps resulted in its repetitiveness. Its appearance was triggered by events in the patient's life that threatened object loss or that dangerously altered the balance of intrapsychic forces by stimulating sexual or aggressive drive derivatives, by weakening defenses (e.g., illness), or by threatening the loss of opportunities for gratification.

Alterations in Mr. A's examination dreams occurred as he achieved mastery of conflict, as the nature of his object relations changed, and as he internalized the representations of controlling and nurturing objects in the course of the analysis. The examiner in his dreams changed from a powerful, judging, critical external object, to a consoling object, to a helpful one, and, finally, to an internalized, reliable aspect of himself.

SUMMARY

A review of the literature on examination dreams and examination anxiety has been made. Support has been offered for the idea that examination dreams are an intermediate form between traumatic dreams and anxiety dreams. A series of dreams from the analysis of a twenty-four-year-old man have been presented, in which the examination dream appeared to reflect an attempt to deal with helplessness, deficient impulse control, and disturbed object relations. The examination dream's form changed as impulses became more effectively controlled and developmental and structural growth took place in the course of the analysis. The notion was advanced that in addition to the examination dream's reassuring function, early problems with impulse control, early experiences with illness and doctors, and intense parental ambivalence about intellectual achievement can be specific factors that influence the choice of this particular form of dream expression.

REFERENCES

Arlow, J.A. (1959). The Structure of the Déjà Vu Experience. *J. Am. Psychoanal. Assoc.* VII pp. 611–631.

Blum, E. (1926). The Psychology of Study and Examinations. *Int. J. Psychoanal.* VII pp. 457–469.

Bonaparte, M. (1947). A Lion Hunter's Dreams. *Psychoanal. Q.* XVI pp. 1–10

Flugel, J.C. (1939). The Examination as Initiation Rite and Anxiety Situation. *Int. J. Psychoanal.* XX pp. 275-286 FREUD 1900 The Interpretation of Dreams. *Standard Edition* IV/V.

Kanzer, M. (1949). Repetitive Nightmares after a Battlefield Killing. *Psychiat. Quarterly Supp.* XXIII pp. 120–126.

Mc Laughlin, J.T. (1961). The Analyst and the Hipprocratic Oath. *J. Am. Psychoanal. Assoc.* IX pp. 106–123.

Sadger, J. (1920). Über Prüfungsangst und Prüfungsträume. *Int. Ztschr. f. Psa.* VII pp. 140–150.

Schmideberg, M. (1933). Ein Prüfungstraum. *Int. Ztschr. f. Psa.* XIX pp. 198–202

Stengel, E. (1936). Prüfungsangst und Prüfungsneurose. *Ztschr. f. Psa. Päd.* X pp. 300–320.

Ward, C.H. (1961). Some Further Thoughts on the Examination Dream. *Psychiat.* XXIV pp. 324–336.

CHAPTER 8

On the Development of the Experience of Mental Self, the Bodily Self, and Self Consciousness

(1971). Psychoanalytic Study of the Child, 26:217–240

IN THIS PAPER I DESCRIBE SOME MATERIAL FROM ANALYTIC PATIENTS that presents a specific pattern of imagery and symptomatology. Using the method of reconstruction, I attempt to demonstrate that this pattern reflects what seems to me to be an underlying archaic body experience which occurs initially as a consequence of separation from mother representatives and which, in similar situations later in life, is regressively activated. I intend to trace its evolution from its beginning in the first year of life to a somewhat less archaic organization indicating some individuation. I hope to add to our "insufficient knowledge" (Freud, 1937) of the early developmental period, when self-object and bodily self-psychic self distinctions appear, and place this addition in the larger framework of the development of consciousness.

CLINICAL MATERIAL

Patient 1

A woman in her 30s suffered from multiple phobias. She could not tolerate buses, trains, tunnels, heights, crowded places, or eating in the presence of others. When she exposed herself to the situations she feared, she felt a confusion that she interpreted as meaning that she was losing her mind. She said she felt she could not control her thoughts. Her greatest fear was that she might vomit. Once she began to vomit she expected to continue to do so, unable to stop, until she died. While having such thoughts, she felt nausea. She could not separate thoughts about nausea and the experience of nausea.

In describing how she felt, she did not often use words such as sad, angry, or embarrassed. Rather, she felt "like a fragile empty bag." Such experiences repeatedly appeared in her dreams. In one, she wandered over a countryside, searching for a place to be alone, but always other people appeared. She found herself in a bathroom, but people wandered in and out. In another, she was driving a car. She drove into a tunnel, the lights went out, she feared she might crash into something, she stopped, someone ran into her car from behind.

In these dreams she seemed to be trying to establish boundaries, attempting to be alone, surrounding herself with bathroom walls, a car, a tunnel—but the need for objects overcame this trend, and she was intruded upon by others. She could not separate herself from objects, yet she feared they would control her and injure her. In fact, she felt she had no will of her own, couldn't initiate things, depended entirely on her husband, following all his suggestions and sharing all his opinions. Yet she feared him and regarded him as a cruel tyrant. She attempted to deal with her problems by isolating herself in her house and, when she was at her worst, in her bedroom in her bed. In

152

her analysis, she tried to contain and control her words and feared she might leak out feces, urine, tears, or vomitus. To her, all these contents were equivalent.

Her symptoms had appeared when she, her husband, and two children established their own home. Prior to this time, they had lived with in-laws, before that with her parents, before that, toward the end of the war, as fugitives. In childhood she had been closely attached to her mother and had regarded her father as an ideal man who could do no wrong. During a temporary separation of her parents (age 9), she had developed a transitory agoraphobia. Earlier (age 5) she had night terrors when her parents went out for the evening.

As an infant she had suffered from an impetigo, which was treated with salves and baths. Toilet training was accomplished by the age of 14 months. The parents were stringent in demanding self-control. When they took her on visits to friends, she was not permitted to indicate a need for a bathroom because her parents regarded this as an unseemly reference to things of which one did not speak. Often she had to restrain herself, painfully and anxiously. Sometimes she failed to do so. "Accidents" were punished by whippings. Tears, expressions of anger or of personal wishes were anathema.

She slept in her parents' bedroom until she was 8 years old. Her father frequently appeared nude, and made the patient sleep nude "for her health." He was seductive with her, both in exciting physical games (wrestling and throwing her in the air), and later, during her mother's frequent depressions, in substituting her for her mother as a companion on walks, theater trips, and café afternoons.

In the analysis, her fears of separation were related to her mother's depressions and the discords between her parents, which gave rise to fears of abandonment. Her response to separation was clarified: it took the form of increased clinging and identification with the abandoning object, accompanied by trends to further regression with fears of explosion, draining, and loss of sense of self. It was proposed that in addition to her uncertain relation to objects, she had experienced skin stimulation that heightened her sense of the surface of her body, in infancy because of her impetigo, later because of beatings and erotic play. It was suggested that excessive stimulation together with early and excessive demands that she contain bodily contents as well as affects led to experiences of painful inner pressure that later reappeared in her experiences of herself as a mass of dangerous contents, held in check by a fragile container. In adult life, the loss of maternal objects that occurred when she felt she must become the mother had been an important factor in precipitating the regressive attempt to recover the object. This reactivated an early state organized in terms of poorly differentiated body surface and interchangeable, dangerous contents, accompanied by absence of feelings of identity and mastery.

Patient 2

A man in his 30s came into analysis shortly after he moved from a job that had clearly defined directives and rigid rules to one that required spontaneity, inventiveness, and an outgoing self-revealing attitude. His success as a bureaucrat had led to his promotion to the position of administrator-consultant. At about the same time, his mother developed heart disease and underwent an operation. He was not aware that this meant something to him. He attempted to attach himself to a superior but failed. Severe anxiety and a moderate depersonalization soon followed. Work became an ordeal. He said he felt that few thoughts or feelings originated with him. In describing his experience of himself, he used such images as feeling like a clam. Someone could reach into his mouth, grab his tongue, and pull out his insides. There he would be, a soft mush. In associating to this imagery, he remembered that in childhood he had felt that his mother knew all his ideas and feelings.

On another day, he said he felt as though encased in armor. He imagined that messages or dagger thrusts could be passed in and out through a chink which was at the same time a source of danger. He felt false—on the surface he was a mask of friendliness; within, a Cassius, hiding in the shadows with a knife.

It became apparent that practically every suggestion or criticism by another person was an intrusion and a blow. This man was always on his guard. Subways and sidewalks were battlegrounds where he constantly risked infringement of his sphere of control. Spontaneity and friendliness were impossible. He feared he might be ridiculed for his friendliness, or his ideas might be taken and used by others. He said he felt like an "insatiably gnawing rat; hiding in a dark corner of [his] interior, ready to spring out when others were not looking, ready to devour what [he] could." He was terrified of injections and rectal examinations. Premature ejaculation or loss of erection sometimes interfered with his ability to penetrate in the sexual act. There was a mild train phobia. Exercising and muscle-conditioning were important because, for him, strong muscles were a protection; they made him feel he had "a casing of cement." He feared crying lest, once started, he be unable to stop; his shell would melt.

Often, at work, he was unable to reveal his ideas and opinions. He feared he had a limited supply of them and might be used and, when empty, discarded. He feared influence and was extremely suggestible. He felt easily exploited. The ideas others had sometimes made him feel "real and warm"; at other times they made him feel he was bursting. Mondays were most difficult because he wanted to stay home, which he said was like being "hidden, protected, warm," as in his childhood when he avoided school.

When he was a child, his mother could always seduce him and arouse him with sexual play. She bathed him until he was 7 or 8. She made him "feel alive." He could not long remain angry with her, even when she hurt or humiliated him. The outside world was "cold and cruel." Mother revealed her body to him, complained to him about his father, kissed him with soft lips. In later life he realized that his desires to perform cunnilingus had to do with these remembered lips. But with his mother he had to respond with sexless affection. Often her friendliness turned to ridicule. Then, he felt "withered," "shrunken," his mind "dried up as though all the juice had dried out of my system." With his mother there was a tremendous temptation to "relax, reveal, loosen." Until the age of 8 or 9, she inspected his bowel movements and praised or derided them as she praised or derided his school performance. He wet himself often. He had had childhood nightmares of being under water, of drowning or suffocating. When excited, he could not control his feelings. Even now, sometimes, as though a switch had flipped, he still changed from "good boy to bad boy, like an erection appearing, from mask to rat."

As an infant he was fed on a rigid schedule, which did not suit him; according to family tradition, he cried in rage for 2 hours before every feeding. Toilet training was undertaken early, but little is known about it. Later he retained stool. Between the ages of 1 and 3, there were almost daily temper tantrums in which he lay screaming and kicking on the floor. He held his breath till he felt he would burst. His mother handled this by letting him tire and get it out of his system. When the patient was 3, his sister was born. For years he had fantasies of killing her. Shortly after her birth, he underwent a tonsillectomy, for which he was unprepared. The sensations of ether anesthesia were included in many subsequent dreams and appeared in waking feelings of suffocation. After this operation the patient was tractable, fearful, and unspontaneous. He imitated others, adapted himself to their standards, and did not create an independent character of his own.

In this case, too, it was evident that the patient's representation of his mother had been disrupted when she fell ill—a disruption that was accentuated with his loss of the maternal elements represented by the large corporation, which provided goals, punishments, nourishment. In response, he first tried to attach himself to a superior; failing in this, he regressed to a level in which an earlier relationship with his mother was partially recaptured. He became unproductive, stayed home, developed a premature ejaculation reminiscent of his enuresis. Tendencies toward more primitive wishes for union with the object appeared. These were evidenced by his fear of and susceptibility to influence. At the same time, there was a reappearance of primitive self experiences involving absence of control and defensively emphasizing the body boundary as a container of undifferentiated internal contents. Feelings, thoughts, secretions were experienced as equivalent. The threat of further dedifferentiation brought about a tendency toward further withdrawal. He felt threatened when "entering" work, trains, or wife, as he felt threatened by others intruding on him, in subways, streets, or competitive situations.

This patient's history revealed, as had that of case 1, events that may have emphasized his sense of surface. There were many references to the erotic relation with mother, the remembered baths, bursting feelings associated with breath holding and stool retention, and banging, kicking, rageful temper tantrums.

Patient 3

Another patient sought reanalysis in his early 40s. He complained of feelings of failure and depression. He said that he had led, and was leading, a false life as a heterosexual because secretly he had homosexual wishes. He experienced strong longings for care and nourishment and rivalrous anger and fear. Meanwhile, he said, he played the role of a human being. He compared his experience of life with the siege of Troy. He wanted to be like an invincible walled city but found himself a hollow Trojan horse as well as susceptible to invasion by one. Troy itself was an imperfect shell, concealing evil. As Troy, as Helen, were entered and controlled, he was easily seduced. A few kind words made him mushy, defenseless. On another occasion he said he felt like an empty paper bag, full of air. A fond hope was one day to be driven in a limousine. This would make him feel safe and protected.

On the analytic couch, he had a number of curious experiences. In one, he felt pressed down, crushed, unable to move. He said it felt as though he were pushed down by a teacup. In association he described tightening feelings in the lips and cheeks and a feeling of pressure on the tongue. During sessions his mouth sometimes began to water as though he were about to eat. He had an urge to pick the skin from his lips, and felt like kicking his feet. A bookcase facing him seemed to swing like a pendulum. He felt sleepy. He was only aware of sensations of surfaces.

He described how, as a child, he had crushed bugs, listening to their shells crack. He had a dream in which, as an oarsman of a shell, he caught a crab. He had a distaste for lobster, and a mild spider phobia. Humpty Dumpty had fascinated him, he remembered, in childhood. He had hoped analysis would be like plastic surgery. He wanted a cosmetic result, an improved surface appearance. He feared anything more extensive than an alteration in the mask because it would involve revealing the worms, the feces inside. There was no experience of solid internal structure, physical or mental. These skeletonless thoughts and feelings seemed to him to represent his real

158

character. Change would involve death. He was reminded of his fear of his mother's anger when he made errors, and this thought reminded him of his fantasy, at age 5, upon hearing her cry in the bathroom, that she had just aborted. He could not imagine change otherwise than in connection with loss of control and death, and this was frightening.

In the transference, he looked for a chink in my armor; he talked of his fear of my rage, which must lie, "like the molten iron beneath the crust of the earth, ready to erupt." In an accident he broke a leg—a strange experience since he had no sense of himself as skeletal. He feared he might soil the couch. On the other hand, he had a wishful fantasy that a hole might be made in his head to let out the pressure of rage, conceived of as a gas or hot liquid. But then, nothing would be left. In sex, he said, the woman sucks the man dry. He becomes an inanimate figure, a dummy. The teacup that pressed him was like the sensation of his mouth around his tongue. Someone could reach into the mouth and take out what he had, or stuff in what he did not want.

This man had had an infantile feeding schedule that was said to have brought him to screams of rage, and a meticulous mother who kept the schedule with iron rigidity. As might be expected, cleanliness, containment of feelings, determined suppression of sexual expressions were demanded. At the same time, the patient slept on a porch adjacent to his parents' bedroom and was over-stimulated and seduced by his mother. He was her intimate, the hearer of her marital complaints, the receiver of her descriptions of the father's inadequacies. Often he felt he would burst with tension and excitement and, until the age of 2½, with the enemas his mother frequently administered.

In this case, too, separation was an important precipitating event in bringing about symptomatology. The first analysis began shortly after his marriage, when he set up his own home, away from his mother. The second analysis came about some years after his mother's death, which he had largely disregarded at the time. Around an anniversary of her death he began to wish for a second child, but his wife refused. This coincided with a change in his work situation, which required him to shift jobs, and his wife's receiving a promotion.

Again, there was a regressive activation of a state in which maintaining a sense of separation and a sense of control were threatened by powerful tendencies toward reunion with an archaic maternal object. In the resultant self experience there was an emphasis on both the surface and a rather undifferentiated interior.

Cases Described in the Literature

Other examples of such self experiences appear in the literature. After Stanley, the 7-year-old patient reported by Elkisch and Mahler (1959), ate some unusually long string beans, he had a delusional obsession in which his body became a sewer as well as the sewer's contents. Teddy, another child, was "preoccupied with the delusion that father, grandfather, and he himself were a communicating system of glass tubes which competed at draining the life fluid from each other during the night" (p. 229). These may represent more primitive variants of the phenomena described by my patients.

A. Reich (1960) reported several cases characterized by a body-phallus equation and pathological self consciousness; one in particular: "When he was little more than six months old, Robert's obsessional mother started toilet training by means of regularly given enemas. For years to come, this interfered with his development of the sense of being a person separate from his mother: it was she who had power over his body. At the same time he experienced himself as an open bag full of excrement" (p. 277). This sense of self as container full of excrement was later included in a body-anal-phallus equation. The later stage was regressively experienced in earlier terms.

Isakower (1938) described certain experiences associated with falling asleep. Among these are sensations particularly in mouth, skin, and hands; sensations of floating, sinking, and giddiness; blurring of the distinction between quite different regions of the body and between internal and external; and visual impressions of an approaching shadowy mass. "The sensations in the oral cavity... are diffused over the whole skin, the outermost frontier of the body, which, indeed, is scarcely yet recognized as such... At all events it represents the surface on which contact is made with the world" (p. 338).

One of Woodbury's patients (1966) felt "hollow," "empty," "without content," "like a person who has lost all his collagen and falls in a puddle" (p. 276).

Winnicott (1962) wrote of a point in the child's developing experience of the self when the surface is experienced as a "limiting membrane" (p. 59). This occurs at a stage in which self-nonself differentiation is taking place.

Lewin (1946), (1953), (1968), Hoffer (1949), Anthony (1961), and Woodbury (1966) also described what they considered to be experiences of reactivated archaic ego states, experiential organizations in which the body experience is mainly centered around the mouth and self-nonself differentiation is incomplete.

Greenacre (1950) reported a comparable case. I excerpt from it briefly.

A woman of thirty sought treatment for severe inhibitions and emotional disturbances invading practically all phases of her life. Extremely shy, sensitive to the point of constant flight from others, she was unable to work for any length of time, and spent much time in idleness, becoming irritable whenever prodded by her family to do anything. [When she

161

was 10, a man lifted her so that she could see the movement of the little hands upon the dials of the gas meter. In doing so] he put his hand under her dress and stimulated her genitals. [Later she allowed herself to be tied up in mock torture. She utilized a technique of masturbating in the bathtub.]... she seemed to be in an unusual state of chronic tension... in almost any situation involving appearance in public,... any special sadomasochistic stimulation (fights or accidents), she would "go to pieces." This meant that she had some sudden spontaneous bodily discharge: a vaginal orgasm, a burst of uncontrolled weeping, loss of control of the bladder, an unexpected diarrhea, or, during her menstrual period, an extreme degree of flooding... at the age of six she was constantly with the mother... as though appersonated by the mother... [She] clung to her bottle until she was about three... She was "successfully" toilet trained extremely early. [She later] lived in a state of fear of toilet accidents... Severe outbursts of temper... were ultimately controlled by whippings... [She experienced] vigorous romping and tickling by her father, and the stimulation of early primal scenes. [Sometimes she] got into states of almost frantic exhilaration. [Dreams revived a memory of (at age 4 or 5) finding her mother doing something to her father's genitals while he was in a plaster cast. Her mother was evidently helping him with a bottle-shaped white-enameled urinal. In kindergarten she had enemas given her in the bathtub. When she had whooping cough, her parents decided to go on vacation anyway, but she was warned not to embarrass the family by coughing or vomiting. A dream in analysis involved getting off a bus in fear of being sick, entering a movie theatre through swinging doors, and going to the toilet. In another part, a little boy put money in a slot machine. Out came hundreds of packages of little cigarettes, and the patient became frightened because the machine was emptying itself] [pp. 206–218].

Kestenberg (1970) and Bornstein (1931) have described similar cases.

DISCUSSION

The material of these patients reveals striking similarities. In their regressed states, they all experienced themselves as what I suggest may be conceptualized as containers and contents. Mental and physical were not distinguished from each other. Instead, thoughts, feelings, concepts were experienced in bodily terms. These patients felt that their bodies consisted of surfaces with openings, through which materials could pass in or out, and of liquid or semiliquid contents. The surface, often shell-like, was described in terms of armor, cement, Troy, the Trojan horse, bugs, the earth's crust, a urinal, bathtub, slot machine, and so on.

The contents—vomitus, flatus, feces, tears, blood, urine, semen, water—were evidently felt and treated as equivalent to crude emotions such as anger and tension, although even as emotions they were still poorly defined, to thoughts, and also to some sense of essence of life. In fantasies incorporating these experiences, drainage could take place and provide relief of tension, but they also threatened dangerous attacks on objects and risks of uncontrolled leakage and death. On the other hand, dangerous fluids, in the form of unwanted foods or injectable substances, and controlling commands arousing dangerous stimuli could be instilled into the container.

An experience of control over input and outflow of these contents was present, but the control was a rudimentary one. The experience of body was not distinct from the experience of mind. Spontaneous activity of all sorts was potentially dangerous and had to be profoundly inhibited. Experiences of falseness were frequent. Strong, undifferentiated attachment to their mothers and precipitation of regression by separation from maternal organizing influences also characterized these patients. Mothers or mother substitutes had to be at least in the background for these patients to feel comfort and personal integrity. The regressive pull involved the wish to recover the maternal object.

The histories of these individuals reveal early influences that evidently brought about intense feelings of body surface and body contents confined by the surface. These early influences, occurring during infancy and the first year of life, included excessive surface and skin stimulation, as described by Greenacre, Hoffer, Winnicott, and others, and, in addition, hollow emptiness due to hunger, and bursting inner pressure due to held breath, or retained feces, and enema fluids. Later in life the parents of these patients exposed them to experiences of the same type, among them seduction and stimulation of feelings and thoughts, especially rage, together with stringent demands for the containment of these mental qualities; similar demands relating to body contents, which thus perpetuated the equation of mental and physical body contents. Separation from mother figures, experienced as abandonment, with the consequent feelings of helplessness and anger, as well as opportunities for spontaneous expression, equated with draining and soiling, resulted in exacerbation of symptomatology. Thinking was in extremes, with rapid switches of attitudes, usually occurring in relation to experiences of hard surface or soft and liquid contents.

These experiences may therefore be thought of as aspects of regressions to fixation points at a stage during which in normal development self-awareness, self-object separation, and mental self-bodily self distinctions begin to occur. The adult phenomenology and observable manifestations reflect the incomplete differentiation of mental and bodily self experience as well as the archaic ties to the object.

CHANGES IN SELF EXPERIENCE IN ANALYSIS

In what follows I shall describe the changes of the bodily self and mental self experiences that occurred during the analyses in my three patients. While many important conflicts and trends were identified and analyzed in the course of these patients' treatment, I restrict myself to the vicissitudes of the organization of early experience and to certain aspects of their relationship to maternal objects.

In patient 1, the phobic woman, the analysis achieved a partial remission of her disabling symptoms. She became able to entertain friends and eat in their company, and, later, even to eat in public. Her sexual interest increased, and her growing sense of control was revealed in an ability to relinquish control in achieving orgasm. The changes in her body experience are of special interest in the present context. She revealed that she had a mild urinary incontinence, a dribbling with sneezing and coughing, which had so frightened her that she had been unable to talk, and even to think, about it. She now decided this might have some anatomic basis, and consulted a physician. She felt she had discovered her anatomy. Her body now felt solid, yet had parts. She had little fear about the vaginal examination and cystoscopy. An uncomplicated operation resulted in a gratifying remission of her symptom, evidently due to parturitional anatomic damage. Later, she adopted a diet and changed her ways of dressing. She became flirtatious in the analysis. Her perception of her body, its functioning, structure, and beauty were expressed in a new hobby.

165

She took up furniture repair and refinishing. She had reached a new stage of self awareness. She began to have sexual daydreams. She became aware of underlying motivations in herself and in others, and recognized a certain degree of complexity in her thoughts. She came to understand, in more than the schematic form she initially had, some of the inner motivations behind her parents' attitudes and behavior. These changes thus brought about a new self awareness and self consciousness, a sense of control and separateness, appreciation of complex motivation in herself and others, and an altered experience of her body.

Patient 2 discovered one day that his attitude about his musculature had changed. He now derived pleasure from the roundness and suppleness of his muscles. Their hardness and armoring quality seemed to him to have lost significance. Subsequently, his golf game became much better as he felt "my body move harmoniously in my swing." Later, he mentioned that he was neglecting a ledger he had carefully kept to record and detail every item of his income and expenses. "After all," he joked, "it's only money." He found himself mentioning ideas to people at work and joking with them, even telling sexual jokes, with a certain retrospective surprise that he had given away something without sense of loss or fear. As one would suppose, his concern about bowels and his worry about adequate sexual performance had markedly diminished. He took to fairly heavy drinking, partly in a spirit of vengeful independence, and partly in a pleasurable exercise of his ability to get high and lose control, as well as for other reasons. His drinking subsided after a while.

Patient 3 presented a complicated analytic development characterized by great variability and changeability. In the context of this paper, one point is noteworthy: the patient repeatedly had tongue-in-mouth experiences reminiscent of the Isakower phenomenon, as well as of Spitz's and Woodbury's comments about the mouth as primal cavity and primal object.

Spitz (1965) says, "all perception begins in the oral cavity" (p. 62), and agrees with Isakower's opinion that sensations in the oral cavity, possibly merged with sensations of the external cutaneous covering, constitute the model for the earliest postnatal ego structure.

Woodbury wrote, "the tongue-in-mouth complex acts not only as a 'screen' but more precisely as a metamorphic framework, referential system, and *perceptual organizer*" (p. 298).

In this patient, the experience of tongue-in-mouth seemed later to have been extended to the total body. It may have contributed to the container-contained experience in the feeling of the body within the teacup and the mind in mental imprisonment, with thought and feeling restriction.

In his analysis, he developed hostile and competitive fantasies frankly put in anal terms. I became shit, and shit less beautiful, less well-formed, and of poorer color than his. He was, he said, frightened by his temerity and elated about his independence in bringing up this thought. He made phallic comparisons, which at that time he assumed would be less favorable to him and consequently more pleasing to me. Often, his manner was one of throwing stones (or fecal pellets) and ducking the response. He separated his thoughts into what he regarded as "good, well-formed ones" and others that were "too liquid, too compressed, or too thrusting." He wondered how to turn his thoughts into money, which he would not spend but store in the bank. He worried that I might become enraged, hurt, intruded upon by his competitiveness. He remembered childhood ideas about his bowel movements. He had daydreams in which, after they were flushed down the toilet, they went into the ground, where they became part of an animated world of little people, serving as furniture, food, and as the little people themselves. In these thoughts the body-cavern was more complex than it had been earlier in his analysis. The intrauterine and anal birth fantasies involved in this thinking became clear to him.

Gradually there appeared an early childhood memory of an enema bag hanging in the bathroom, then memories of baths with mother, enemas, his fear he might not be able to hold in the water and thus anger his mother, her coldness, his need for closeness. He competed with me in the area of interpretations, tried to make them first, and read analytic literature. Fears of separation and of the effects of his anger led to tearful thoughts about accidents, his son's health, dreams involving dismemberment and blood, and a variety of phallic castration anxiety components, as well as to frequent returns to the earlier, simpler shell in which the interior was undifferentiated.

At this stage, the similarity of this case to classical descriptions of anal conflict seen as regressions from phallic conflicts stands out. The anatomic and concurrent mental experience and the transference relationship were obviously interrelated. The patient's thinking style and other mental organizations showed a clear relationship to the associated organization of body experience and object relationships.

To sum up the clinical evidence: these patients initially demonstrated a container-containment self experience which in the course of analysis changed. In two cases, a differentiation of the surface and the interior of the body appeared. Patient 2 came to feel his muscles, which developed volume and synergism. He lost his sense that things taken in or let out were directly, quantitatively related to the extent to which he was alive and powerful. As his body surface came to be experienced as subdivided, no longer uniform, so did what went in and out.

The woman patient became aware of a liquid-containing cavern within her body. A bladder appeared as a part of her body. Her sense of her body now included curves and volumes as well as surfaces, pleasure-giving orifices and subdivisions of organs as well as inlets and outlets. She played with anatomy in her furniture restorations. Her thoughts and feelings became more separated from each other and from early body experience, and could be dealt with as things apart, abstracted, to be played with or allowed to have existences of their own, so to speak, just as the body and its contents were subdivided, more subtly experienced, something possessed.

Play with the body in golf, sexual relations, and with the mind in having an alcoholic high, or a daydream, appeared in these patients' lives, together with the experience of a superordinate sense of control of the self which was separable into bodily self and mental self components.

Coincidentally with the developments just mentioned, both patients noticed a certain separation from their archaic mothers and maternal representatives. With this separation came a sense of independence and the capacity to think about their mothers in a more abstract, observant way. Both patients showed a new awareness of their mothers as individuals with minds and consciousnesses. Regressions, terrors, and rages in relation to these figures diminished, to be replaced by less automatic (in Hartmann's sense [1939]) responses. Of course, fluctuations and regressions continued to occur. Spiegel (1970) discusses comparable changes in analytic patients and terms them developments from "perceptual" to "cognitive ego." Modell (1968) believes that such behavior in analysis reflects mental organizations characteristic of the development period of the "transitional object," which precedes that of "the sense of identity."

The third patient showed a number of levels of organization, including tongue-in-mouth, container-contained, organ and mental differentiation, and more subtle awarenesses on a phallic level. In this case the patient's analytic experience seemed to recapitulate and rework stages in his ontogenesis.

169

The Early Organization in the Sequence of Development

I think it is reasonable to suggest that the two main organizations just described—the container-contained, and the segmented, partly differentiated body—and their associated experiences of mental activity can be located within a larger ontogenetic sequence. The body sequence would be: (1) a hypothetical undifferentiated stage such as that described by Bak;[1] (2) the mouth, or mouth-tongue organization; (3) the container-contained stage; (4) the period of developing experience of organ, orifice, and surface differentiation. In the container-contained stage, there begins to be an awareness of the body, separate from diffuse mental experience. This is followed by an awareness of more differentiated thoughts and feelings separate from concrete body experience. Eventually, there appear thoughts divorced from body experience as well as the capacity to distinguish between different types of mental experience. For example, a child in the early phallic phase can identify a dream and distinguish it from other thoughts or real events.

A 3½-year-old child's dog died.[2] Days later, she awoke in the morning and told her mother that she had dreamed that she and her nurse had gone to buy another dog. Some hours later, the child asked the nurse if she remembered going to buy the dog. When the nurse looked puzzled, the child brightened and remembered, "Oh yes, it

---

1 Bak (1939), (1943) reviewed a number of phenomena encountered in schizophrenics. These included experiences of cosmic significance, fusion, self-object confusions, and temperature sensitivity. He suggested that rapid cooling of the baby after delivery might contribute to the thermal orientation of schizophrenics, and that temperature sensations may be the earliest body experiences, before self-nonself differentiation occurs. Separation from the object reactivates the early experiences of separation from mother, and loss of warmth leads to a subsequent frozen world feeling.

2 For a further discussion of the development of dream recognition, see Greenacre (1964), especially pp. 12-14.

was a dream." There was a suspension of what Schafer (1968) calls the reflective self representation, that is, of the distinction between mental and bodily self experience with a superordinate self-observer, and its later reinstitution. A capacity for awareness of dream experience, involving a self-observation and a distinction between mental self, bodily self, and nonself was at this time becoming established in this little girl. This may be called self consciousness. The dream within the dream is a representation, in the dream, of the waking experience of dream recognition. The dream within the dream means one has recognized a dream as a dream, in the waking state. It is a late occurrence and constitutes evidence of an experience of mind. In this case there is thought about thought, consciousness of consciousness. This is self-self consciousness, an aspect of a relatively advanced organizational stage.

A dream reported by patient 2 late in his analysis contained representations of a number of self and object experiences he had previously described at various times. It can serve to illustrate a model of ontogenetic experiences eventually leading to self-self consciousness. In this dream, the patient observed an execution. A queen ordered the condemned criminal to stand. He did, and an executioner struck him on the back with an axe. The patient (as observer in the dream) experienced both a feeling that this was inevitable and amazement that the criminal had no awareness or understanding of the meaning of this fate, that is, of the permanence of death. In analyzing this dream, the patient recalled that his mother had punished transgressions in a ritualistic manner, commanding him to get the hairbrush, lower his trousers, and bend over her knees. Then the punishment was meted out. It never occurred to him to rebel. He could not conceive of the idea, "I can prevent her doing this to me." It was inevitable. Now he could look back on himself at this period, from a new viewpoint, that of the amazed observer.

The representation of the robotlike prisoner who has almost no self experience is a representation of a "reminiscence" of the early organizational stage in which separation from mother is incomplete. All things come from her. The object's commands equal the subject's response.

The patient as amazed dream observer is a representation of an organization that includes an experience of a mental self separate from and controlling a bodily self. Bodily pain and passivity are experienced as different from mental pain and passivity. This organization developed later in the patient's life than the early organization, referred to in the dream, to which it is contrasted. In the analytic hour the patient was a waking observer who described the dream observer, who in turn, from a separated viewpoint, observed the queen who controlled the mindless, acquiescent prisoner.

Another association was the idea that he and his mother had both wished he were, and thought of him as, her phallus. This wishful fantasy of the phallic stage combined the phallic wish with the archaic wishes for union with mother, and was expressed in the regressive terms of early experience. It included the experience the patient had of himself as a container, attached to his mother. As with A. Reich's patients, very early experiences entered into a much later body-phallus fantasy. Schuster (1969) reported a patient with a body-phallus identification who on the couch experienced a feeling of increasing size. This patient traced the feeling back only as far as latency when it had entered into the body-phallus identification. A much earlier origin is likely.

The dream and its treatment in the analysis thus include representations from a developmental series of experiences of the self. These are: (1) an un-self experiencing mind-body almost equated with the object, the prisoner; (2) the experiencing prisoner in his containerlike, blood-containing aspect, experiencing crude emotions, and being controlled by the queen; (3) the dream observer of this situation experiencing the subtler emotion, amazement, and recognizing the separation between the prisoner and the queen; (4) the self-conscious patient aware of his role as inventor and reporter of the dream; and (5) the self-self-conscious, waking observer of the dream inventor and invention. (In the last, the patient is aware of himself as observer of his and his mother's mutually shared fantasy of being mother's phallus.)

These are organizations that involve increasingly general, abstract, and inclusive self and object experiences. The most subtle includes self consciousnesses of the mental self. They represent steps in the history of the patient's self-self consciousness development. A further abstraction took place later on, when the patient imagined himself as the analyst observing all this. Spiegel (1970) termed this a development to "the cognitive self."

A parallel development sequence of bodyself experience might be: (1) primal state of undifferentiation; (2) container-contained; (3) orifice and some organ awareness with differentiated surface and interior separate from waste products and secretions and with some sense of control over the liquid contents; (4) mind awareness, with mind differentiated as a psychic organ controlling differentiated body organs and their contained materials; (5) consciousness of awareness of mind.

A parallel object relation sequence can also be constructed: (1) fusion; (2) self and object distinction, in which the self remains attached, appendagelike to the object, which is in control; (3) objects including organs are distinguished, persist in memory in the absence of external stimuli, and are manipulable in fantasy; (4) awareness of (3) as in the controlled daydream; and (5) consciousness of the object's and the self's awareness and fantasies.

173

These sequences are consistent with Mahler's views. Mahler (1968) describes two subphases within the phase of primary narcissism, absolute primary narcissism followed in the third month by the symbiotic stage. The first phase "is marked by the infant's lack of awareness of a mothering agent." In the second, "the infant begins dimly to perceive need satisfaction as coming from a need-satisfying part object—albeit still from within the orbit of his omnipotent symbiotic dual unity with a mothering agency" (p. 10). In this second substage the "body ego contains two kinds of self representations: there is an inner core of the body image, with a boundary that is turned toward the inside of the body and divides it from the ego; and an outer layer of sensoriperceptive engrams, which contributes to the boundaries of the 'body self.'... the shift of predominantly proprioceptive-enteroceptive cathexis toward sensoriperceptive cathexis of the periphery is a major step in development" (p. 11).

Later in this symbiotic subphase (overlapping with the separation-individuation phase at about 12 to 18 months), the "body is taken as object... with the well-known focal concentration on the libidinal zones" (Elkisch and Mahler, 1959, p. 219). Greenacre (1953) feels that until the age of about 6 months, "the mouth and lips," "tactile sensations," "superficial kinesthetic responses," and "smell" furnish the bulk of the sensory life of the infant, with hearing and vision playing extremely variable roles. With the development of sitting up, focusing of the eyes, and more precise arm and hand movements, much of the infant's exploratory activity is switched from mother to prehensile vision and arm-hand activity. Mahler's "hatching period" beginning in the last quarter of the first year of life blends with Greenacre's stage after 6 months. There is a shift, Mahler writes, toward "sensoriperceptive cathexis" involving concentration on the libidinal zones and the body experiences occurring with more precise arm and hand movements. The patterns and transitions regressively re-experienced by the patients described presumably appear in this period and can be considered aspects of it.

Greenacre (1964), as noted before, discusses the age at which a child recognizes his dreams as such; upon reviewing the data of others as well as her own, she concluded this may occur in the 4th year. Greenacre also quotes a 4½-year-old child saying of God, "He is *not real*. God is just thinking" (p. 13). God's thoughts are apparently equivalent to dream reality, and distinguished from waking reality.

My example supports the view that children of this age distinguish between psychic reality and external reality. I have no data to suggest the normal age at which self-self consciousness may first appear.

SUMMARY

There are understandable doubts that conclusions drawn about early development from phenomena of later life are correct, and that normal development can be deduced from pathological manifestations. Nevertheless, numerous authors have made plausible suggestions about early development based on observations of phenomena seen in analytic patients in later life. Certain patients respond to the loss of real or internal objects with a regressive dedifferentiation characterized by the loss of a clear sense of self. They feel controlled by others and have self experiences in which mind-body distinctions are weakened, and in which affects and physical elements are crudely and not separately experienced. At the same time, their regressive response involves an attempt to regain the object on a more primitive level and to maintain the separated self. This new balance is unstable, containing the threat of further regression to a still more dedifferentiated state in which self-object distinctions may be lost.

In their imagery, these patients reveal a self experience in which the self is composed of a potentially permeable container, rather uniform, sometimes hard or brittle, and sometimes fragile, and contents made up of thoughts, feelings, and fluids that are poorly distinguished from each other. This container with its contents threatens to become attached to and controlled by an object similarly poorly defined and differentiated. This self experience seems to involve the reactivation of early sensations caused by skin stimulation, breath holding, fecal and enema fluid retention, and feelings of rage and tension. The history given by these patients includes numerous occasions when such experiences must have occurred.

This organization seems more developed than the oral state discussed by Spitz and Woodbury, but clinically one may observe the fear of further regressions, particularly the fear of an objectless selfless state.

In the course of analysis a more differentiated experience of self and objects appears. The experience of a uniform body surface and contents is replaced by an experience of a body made up of organs having distinct and differing characters. Mental contents are also more clearly distinguished from body experiences and from each other. Affects are more differentiated and motives and thoughts are separately perceived. In addition, an experience of observation appears. Objects as well as body and mental self are observed. Spiegel (1970p. 688) describes this as the establishment of a "cognitive self" which reaches "beyond the present into the past... yet retaining the present" and that includes self and object perceptions. This development may be viewed as a part of normal development taking place between 12 and 18 months of age in the evolution from the archaic objectless state to the mature organization when self-self consciousness is established.

REFERENCES

Anthony, E.J. (1961). A Study of "Screen Sensations." *Psychoanal. Study Child* 16:211–245.

Bak, R.C. (1939). Regression of Ego-Orientation and Libido in Schizophrenia *Int. J. Psychoanal.* 20:64–71.

——— (1943). Dissolution of the Ego, Mannerism, and Delusion of Grandeur *J. Nerv. Ment. Dis.* 98 457–463.

Bornstein, B. (1931). Phobia in a Two-and-a-Half-Year-Old Child *Psychoanal. Q.* 4:93–119 1935.

Elkisch, P. & Mahler, M.S. (1959). On the Infantile Precursors of the "Influencing Machine" (Tausk) *Psychoanal. Study Child* 14:219–235

Freud, S. (1905). Jokes and Their Relation to the Unconscious. *Standard Edition* 8 London: Hogarth Press, 1960.

——— (1937) Constructions in Analysis. *Standard Edition* 23:255-269 London: Hogarth Press, 1964.

Greenacre, P. (1941). The Predisposition to Anxiety In: *Trauma, Growth and Personality.* New York : International Universities Press, 1969 pp. 27–82.

——— (1945). The Biological Economy of Birth In: *Trauma, Growth and Personality.* New York: International Universities Press, pp. 3–26.

——— (1948). Anatomical Structure and Superego Development In: *Trauma, Growth and Personality.* New York: International Universities Press, pp. 149–164.

——— (1950). The Prepuberty Trauma in Girls In: *Trauma, Growth and Personality.* New York: International Universities Press, pp. 204–223.

——— (1953). Certain Relationships between Fetishism and the Faulty Development of the Body Image. *Psychoanal. Study Child* 8:79–98.

——— (1964). A Study on the Nature of Inspiration. *J. Am. Psychoanal. Assoc.* 13:6–31.

Hartmann, H. (1939). *Ego Psychology and the Problem of Adaptation.* New York: International Universities Press, 1958.

——— (1950). Comments on the Psychoanalytic Theory of the Ego. *Psychoanal. Study Child* 5:74–96.

Hoffer, W. (1949). Mouth, Hand and Ego-Integration *Psychoanal. Study Child* 3/4:49–56.

Isakower, O. (1938). A Contribution to the Patho-Psychology of Phenomena Associated with Falling Asleep *Int. J. Psychoanal.* 19:331–345

Jacobson, E. (1954). The Self and the Object World *Psychoanal. Study Child* 9:75–127

——— (1964). *The Self and the Object World.* New York: International Universities Press.

Kestenberg, J.S. (1970). Discussion of "The Transitional Object and the Fetish" by Phyllis Greenacre, New York Psychoanalytic Society.

Lewin, B.D. (1946). Sleep, the Mouth, and the Dream Screen *Psychoanal. Q.* 15:419–34.

——— (1953). Reconsideration of the Dream Screen *Psychoanal. Q.* 22:174–199.

——— (1968). *The Image and the Past New York:* International Universities Press.

Mahler, M.S. & Furer, M (1968). *On Human Symbiosis and the Vicissitudes of Individuation.* New York: International Universities Press.

Modell, A.H. (1968). *Object Love and Reality.* New York: International Universities Press.

Reich, A. (1960). Pathologic Forms of Self-Esteem Regulation. *Psychoanal. Study Child* 15:215–232.

Schafer, R. (1968). *Aspects of Internalization.* New York: International Universities Press.

Schilder, P. (1935). *The Image and Appearance of the Human Body.* New York: International Universities Press, 1950.

——— (1942). *Mind: Perception and Thought in Their Constructive Aspects.* New York: Columbia University Press.

Schuster, D.B. (1969). Bisexuality and Body as Phallus *Psychoanal. Q.* 38:72–80

Spiegel, L.A. (1970). The Self, Reality and Perception. *Ann. N.Y. Acad. Sci.* 169 683–694.

Spitz, R.A. & Cobliner, W.G. (1965). *The First Year of Life.* New York: International Universities Press.

Winnicott, D.W. (1962). The Aims of Psycho-Analytical Treatment. In: *The Maturational Processes and the Facilitating Environment.* New York: International Universities Press, (1965). pp. 166–170.

Woodbury, M.A. (1966). Altered Body-Ego Experiences: A Contribution to the Study of Regression, Perception, and Early Development. *J. Am. Psychoanal. Assoc.* 14:273–303.

BOOK REVIEWS

BOOK REVIEWS

CHAPTER 9

The Hartmann Era

(2004). *Psychoanalytic Quarterly,* 73(3):836–851
Edited by Martin S. Bergmann, Ph.D. New York: Other Press, 2000. 374 pp.

Under the aegis of the Psychoanalytic Research and Development Fund, Martin Bergmann organized a conference with the title of "The Hartmann Era," and invited nine other senior analysts to prepare contributions as responses to his precirculated introductory review paper, "The Hartmann Era and Its Contribution to Psychoanalytic Technique." All the papers were then discussed among the conferees, and were published in 2000 as the subject book.

In addition to Bergmann, the invited authors who presented papers included Jacob Arlow, Harold Blum, André Green, William Grossman, Otto Kernberg, Anton Kris, Peter Neubauer, Albert Solnit, and Clifford Yorke. Two officers of the fund, Mortimer Ostow and Sidney Furst, made comments as well.

The most general conclusion, supported more or less by all, was that Hartmann had made a number of significant contributions, some of which have essentially been found useful, others not, and others still—in the opinion of a majority of contributors, at least—were deleterious to psychoanalytic clinical and theoretical progress. All the prepared contributors were well known for their many publications and discussions, and all had interesting points of view, many of which had been extensively presented elsewhere. Yorke, Neubauer, and Solnit had had extensive working and personal contact with Hartmann, and

183

Grossman less so; Kris was a member of the family, and the others had read the literature of the time without, I think, having had direct contact with the various authors chiefly under discussion. None were historians.

Most of the authors deemed that there was a period of time in the United States when Hartmann and his contemporaries, mainly European immigrants to New York, formed a group with a generally common approach to psychoanalysis. The conference members noted that there was a divergence of interests and approaches among these "Hartmannites" (a conference neologism) during the "Hartmann Era" (another neologism). But the similarities of their attitudes bound them together, and their collective influence was, for a time, dominant in American analysis, though not elsewhere. The impression of Hartmannian dominance was general in the comments of blurb writers Robert Michels and Robert Wallerstein, as well as in the meeting participants, but most of the comments supporting this conclusion were made by people too young or too far from New York to have had significant direct contact with the protagonists.

Another point made was that the Hartmann Era has ended, as evidenced by the fact that Hartmann is rarely taught, read, or cited these days. I believe the intended inference to be that the work of the Hartmannites, not only that of Hartmann himself, is not deemed to have much to offer to today's psychoanalytic scene.

I noticed that most of the citations by the participants were to themselves or to other participants. I missed the use of a comparison group. Much of the interest of the participants was, understandably, not only in commenting about the historical period under discussion, but also in presenting their own thoughts and ideas about psychoanalysis. For instance, Kris explained his ideas about conflict, while Green presented an impressive discussion of his belief that conflicted, drive-driven, unconscious inner life is communicated by the mother to her infant. He explained that infant observation, which cannot take such undeterminable but profoundly significant factors into account, is psychoanalytically useless, since observation cannot reveal what is going on in the mind.

But where is the data to support the notion that the Hartmann epoch saw a hegemony that excluded others' ideas to the extent that the speakers maintained? That there was a Hartmann era, and that the Hartmannites dominated American psychoanalysis, is an arguable proposition, but it was not argued at this conference. Instead, it seems to me, in addition to the interesting views expressed, a good deal of misunderstanding and a good deal of ad hominem attack were in evidence.

How does the current lack of attention to these writers resemble or differ from the fate of previous generations? Who reads the second-generation Freudian inner circle now? What happened to the interest in Rank, Abraham, and Jones? Or Schilder? Or even Ferenczi? Who reads Ferenczi (though it would be hard to assert that Ferenczi does not live on in interpersonalist thinking)? And why is that so? And if it is so, what does this mean?

How much are Margaret Mahler, Edith Jacobson, Rudolf Loewenstein and Ernst Kris, Anna Freud, Rene Spitz, Annie Reich, Robert Bak, and others—all termed "Hartmann followers"—read, taught, and cited, and what is the significance of this, sixty years after the publication of *Ego Psychology and the Problem of Adaptation?* Why are Jansky and de Hirsch unmentioned, given that they were pioneers of children›s psychological testing, an area that has continued to develop, and has led to profound effects on education and to a greater understanding of cognitive functioning? Nor has there been further consideration of the active interest in adolescence and later childhood that was encouraged by the Hartmann group, or its effects on clinical attitudes toward people who had previously been traditionally treated as obstinate and resistive.

With the exception of Arlow, Neubauer, Grossman, Solnit, and Yorke, the other participants had much to say about how the dominance they believe occurred had harmed those then excluded from the inner circle (Klein especially, Lacan to some extent, Nunberg perhaps) and impeded analytic progress (which Kernberg thought had cost us twenty years by delaying otherwise possible advances) by their hegemony. Green thought Bertram Lewin had fallen into oblivion because his ideas were not acceptable to the ruling group. Kernberg thought Winnicott was not heard because he was regarded as Kleinian.

As to hegemony, Arlow noted that *The Psychoanalytic Study of the Child* was founded and edited by Hartmann and his close associates,[3] but that *The Journal of the American Psychoanalytic Association* was not. The editorial board of the latter had one possible Hartmannite, Sam Ritvo, as well as a probable one, Max Schur. Arlow, Kenneth Calder, Edward Joseph, and Heinz Kohut were also included. *The Psychoanalytic Quarterly's* editors included a friend of Hartmann, Alex Bromley, as well as Lewin, Arlow, David Beres, Lawrence Kubie, and Karl Menninger—but no Hartmannites.

Arlow felt that the Hartmann period ended when Hartmann failed to counter the arguments of philosopher Sidney Hook. In a famous discussion, Hook said that, whenever one cannot say what would have happened if a particular phenomenon had not occurred (in this case, the Oedipus complex, which was claimed to be universal), then one cannot claim anything for the so-called phenomenon itself. Hartmann failed to respond. Who could counter such a proposition?

---

3 I note that in the arbitrarily chosen year, 1967, Lewin—one of those said to be excluded—was actually an editor of *The Psychoanalytic Study of the Child.*

Some years later, I had a conversation with Hook myself, and he stated the same principle. I asked if he had a son. "Yes," he replied. I asked if he had noticed that his relationship with his son was more competitive and difficult than the son's relationship with his mother. "Yes," said Hook. I asked if this was something he had noticed among his acquaintances; "yes," said Hook. "That's the Oedipus Complex," I said. "Oh," said Hook. "No one ever put it that way before." Who now reads or has even heard of Hook?

I believe that Hartmann's contemporaries—and probably even his collaborators, Ernst Kris and Loewenstein—thought that they were making original contributions in their own ways, whether in collaboration with him or independently, and would not like to have been termed Hartmannites. But to return to the crucial point: Was there or was there not a Hartmann Era—an era of dominance, of exclusionary hegemony of Hartmann's ego psychology—that led to the useless lengthening of analyses and to the deterioration of interest in and significance of psychoanalysis? Did such an era really exist, responsible for twenty lost years of progress, for the silencing of dissenting voices, for making extravagant promises that led to disappointment?

I had the good fortune to have been trained in psychiatry at Albert Einstein College of Medicine in New York, at that time the most exciting place to be because of the wide diversity of teaching. Among my teachers were Morton Reiser, then already thick into the study of psychophysiology; Ed Hornick, a rather interpersonal eclectic; Emanuel Ghent, a Horneyan-Sullivanian; and Robert Bak and Andrew Peto, Freudians. Israel Zwerling was a social activist, and many others whose interests and research varied enormously had ample opportunity to present their views to anyone interested enough to listen. Sybil Escalona was doing child observation aimed at making prospective conclusions about child development. Wagner Bridger, a Pavlovian, and others of all persuasions were invited to come and teach, and they did so.

We read Sullivan, Horney, Klein, Fromm-Reichman, and others. We heard about "active" therapy of schizophrenics from John Rosen, who claimed to cure schizophrenia. Rosen demonstrated his approach in attempted interviews with a silent schizophrenic patient-who, Rosen knew, liked to suck on used sanitary napkins—by telling him that he knew about his habit, and that his silence and sucking showed he was a "mouth case." Rosen said he had punched another patient who had made a suicide attempt, saying, "Don›t ever do that to me again," and that he had hidden outside the room where still another patient was sleeping, awakening him by banging on his window from outside and yelling, "Now can you tell the difference between a noise and a hallucination?"

We heard about and read Franz Alexander. Sandor Rado explained that the Egyptian pyramids had been built to ensure that dead people could not come back, and that ambivalence was not involved. We read that Melitta Sperling claimed to have cured ulcerative colitis and other so-called psychosomatic diseases. We heard about schizophrenogenic mothers and double-binds. I do not feel that we were insulated from the wide variety of then-active approaches and attempts to try to help sicker people. We—and, of course, patients and their families—were subsequently disappointed and angry about what later seemed to have been failed and insulting experiments, presented with passionate belief by their practitioners, but without evidence of efficacy.

I was a psychoanalytic candidate at New York Psychoanalytic Institute between 1962 and 1966, while I taught and researched at Einstein, and I had the opportunity to meet, study with, and to befriend many senior analysts of the time. They included Victor Rosen, Arlow, Charles Brenner, Jacobson, Mahler, Phyllis Greenacre, Grace Abbate, Marianne Kris, Charles Fisher, Kurt and Ruth Eissler,

Berta Bornstein, Loewenstein, Lillian Malcove, Otto Isakower, Leo Stone, Bak, and Hartmann himself. Of course, I also knew the next generation—Martin Stein, for instance—as well as the generation after that—Milton Horowitz and Manuel Furer, to name two.

As for Winnicott, his works were taught—and well taught—when I was a student, and when he came to speak, the crowd that came to hear him literally spilled into the street. In addition, there were quite a number of Lewinians, including Kubie, Isakower, and Malcove; Lewin's Freud lecture and other speeches were greatly admired. His dream course was probably the most respected and talked about at the institute, and his books were widely read. Arlow and Brenner were certainly irrepressible, and they were certainly not Hartmannites.

At that time, I noted that a number of interpersonal factors were active at the New York Psychoanalytic. There was hot competition between some who were natives of the United States and others who were immigrants, with significant envy and resentment on the part of some Americans toward the Europeans. There was significant resentment on the part of members of both groups toward those on the education committee who conferred training analyst status. This was hardly an unusual situation; however, the body that made those decisions could be described as a clique only by stretching the data, given that Europeans made up nearly half of its members. The faculty was probably more heterogeneous than most, but this did little to temper political and personal feelings.

- Hartmann, in this book, is described as coming from an "aristocratic" background and as one-quarter Jewish. No one else was ethnically described or pigeonholed according to social class.
- He is criticized because he did not involve himself in larger causes than those he wrote about.

▶ He is criticized because he never became involved with more than a narrow population of relatively normal people (though his first paper included an explanation of how the confabulations of those with Korsakoff›s psychosis could be understood from a psychodynamic viewpoint). He did not concern himself with borderlines or psychotics.

▶ He is criticized for not having written about the Nazis or the Holocaust. Blum wrote, "The theoretical concept of the average expectable environment... courted science fiction," and that "adaptation" meant "compliance with the Nazis" (p. 94). Hartmann (1960) once wrote that "The sociocultural environment has a positive share in the establishment of moral behavior. But it is also true that relative freedom from sociocultural pressure runs parallel with the development of the superego" (p. 39), and that "The high value placed on the facing and acceptance of outer and inner reality" and "'acceptance' of reality... [do] not imply, in the context of analytic thinking, passive submission to a given social system" (p. 89).[4]

▶ Supposedly, according to Bergmann, the Hartmannites recommended that secondarily autonomous character traits should not be analyzed. Where is this recommendation to be found?

▶ Hartmann›s work is criticized because he failed to relate his theories to specific clinical examples and problems. This criticism, occurring thirty year later, amounts to Monday morning quarterbacking.

---

4 Hartmann, H. (1960). *Psychoanalysis and Moral Values*. New York: Int. Univ. Press.

▸ Hartmann and his group were said to have excluded others.[5]

▸ Among transplanted Europeans, there was gossip about this or that refugee›s having been sent to Cleveland or Pittsburgh or some other place because "there are enough analysts in New York." How seriously are we meant to take personal criticisms and statements about how people should have behaved and what they should have done in their lives? Is this appropriate at a scientific meeting?

▸ A certain degree of clannishness seems to me to have been expectable among those who had grown up in one cultural milieu, lost it, and then had to deal with transplantation.

▸ At the New York Psychoanalytic Institute, an American, largely female leadership was indeed succeeded by a largely European one, which was, in turn, held to be an arrogant gerontocracy, and was attacked and eventually replaced by a more "democratic" group—which in turn was attacked and replaced. Such rivalries and their political expressions were— and are, of course— ubiquitous.

Much of this was affectionately and satirically described in a series of *New Yorker* stories featuring Al Blauberman, Selboat Selzer, and others, written by Lillian Ross. But that was then (in the mid-1960s) and this is now, and it is surprising to find such attitudes expressed by eminent colleagues at the present time.

Hartmann's writings, as everyone agrees, are difficult, to say the least. His ideas meandered; he made connections that led to deviations from the main topic. Often, these digressions were interesting in themselves, though not directly related to the expectations one might

---

5 For Kernberg's statements related to this point, see p. 229 and pp. 285-286 of the subject book.

have from the title of a particular essay. Hartmann himself was fully aware of this, pointed it out, and often noted that he had brought up a matter more suitable for another discussion. In addition, his sentence structure was difficult for readers to follow; mostly, I think, his mind was full of ideas and thoughts, and his writings all had an important aspect: the complexity of human thinking and the multiplicity of levels on which it takes place. His writing style exemplifies the problem of reducing extravagant complication to relatively simple, understandable statements. But he could also be quite clear, as, for example, in the following quotation:

> The recognition of acts of moral evaluation, and of their imperative character as dynamically relevant, often decisive, aspects of the personality, is part of self-knowledge in the same way as is the recognition of the instinctual drives and their aims in the id, and the recognition of the aims and functions of the ego.[6]

These words probably represent Hartmann's attempt to systematize his viewpoint (for which he was criticized by those who felt it caused rigidification), which was also evident in his discussions of neutralization, deneutralization, and related topics, carried out in a somewhat obsessive way, when he knew perfectly well that he was discussing a purely suppositional subject. But Hartmann had reasons for doing this. He wanted a way to explain change in the presence of constancy, and that required some concept of what remained constant, or at least how constancy can be regarded, and he took the drives as that constant. How could a person be the same person

---

6 Hartmann, H. (1960). *Psychoanalysis and Moral Values*. New York: Int. Univ. Press, p. 41.

throughout life and still change so much? One's physiology changes, the mental capacities change, the environment changes, functions change, childhood dependency is largely left behind—and yet, the same person is continuous.

Hartmann did not resolve this question, and neither, to my mind, has anyone else. I note, however, that his theorizing about drives was an attempt to emphasize the significant and basic biological-ness of mental functioning. So was his interest in proposing the idea of autonomous ego functions, which to him were also rooted in biology. None of this supports the idea, often mentioned in the past and at this conference, that Hartmann abandoned biological rootedness and substituted an excessive emphasis on reality.

The same can be said for another frequent criticism of Hartmann: that his adaptation was a kind of submission to external forces and institutions. For instance, the opinion was expressed by some at this conference that he diminished the importance of the struggle against the social forces that impinge on individuals. Hartmann›s idea was that social institutions are used to serve psychic needs, and that they often need to be opposed and altered in order to serve these needs.

To me, his consistent efforts to deal with the extraordinary complexity of psychic life in relation to biological, contextual, social, and interpersonal forces were the most important aspect of his work. In his earlier days in Vienna, when he worked as a ward chief and spent hours at cafés with house officers, he had the reputation of being a brilliant clinician and diagnostician, as well as an inspiring teacher.

I do not think that Hartmann could have come up with a simple, useful though limited, organizing idea, such as unconscious fantasy, strain trauma, compromise formation, personal myth, or the death instinct. He was no Freud, Klein, Lacan, or Kohut, nor a Sterba, Rado, or Katan. He abhorred the idea of wise-man leadership that included a retinue of enthusiastic followers, and made no effort to create such a scene.

Because of the difficulties in understanding Hartmann's writings, a group working on a variety of research problems (Morton Reiser, Alan Tyson, Herb Weiner, William Grossman, Bob Kabcinell, and Gene Goldberg), invited Hartmann to come to Montefiore, in the Bronx, to discuss his ideas over a series of long meetings. Since I was fortunate enough to hear his discussion—and given the rest of my background in the 1950s, ⊠60s, and ⊠70s, as described above—I was not prepared for some of what I read in this book describing the Hartmann Era conference.

Notwithstanding the presentation at Montefiore, Hartmann did not really discuss his ideas very much in public. He acted like a shy and diffident person. He muttered asides to whoever was sitting beside him at presentations of papers. Often, these asides amounted to corrections of a presenter's mistake in citing the source of an idea of Freud's. He mumbled while turning his head away from the microphone. He disliked public controversy, perhaps partly because of his state of health (he had already suffered heart attacks), and probably partly out of a dislike of what often became a heated argument. No doubt all this added to an impression of him as aloof and arrogant. He was held responsible for the appointment of his wife as a training analyst, provoking resentment. These factors, as well as his dislike of the idea of creating a following, militated against his work's being well understood.

Finally, and perhaps most important, Hartmann was ill for a long period and died at age seventy-five, in 1970. His career in New York had lasted twenty-nine years, many of them characterized by depleted energy. He missed opportunities to clarify, to discuss, to refute his critics, and to further refine his ideas. He was certainly not responsible for some of the more obsessional attempts of those who tried to reify his characteristically allusive and many-leveled thinking. I do not think anyone who knew Hartmann would have regarded him as a linear thinker, although there were some who proposed classifying his approach as linear.

Nevertheless, I was surprised by the misconceptions of many of the contributors to this conference. First, although Hartmann was privileged, he was no aristocrat. He came from an upper-bourgeois, liberal, intellectual background, and had an educational and cultural background similar to those of others of his time— gymnasium, university, medical school. He was not a slacker in going to Switzerland, as someone implied (and as Anton Kris refuted). He was a Swiss citizen and proud of it. Dora Hartmann converted to Swiss Calvinism so that she could be buried with him in the Fextal near Sils Maria, near Nietzsche, in a place where the Hartmanns had spent part of every summer vacation.

Perhaps there is an anti-intellectual, politically leftist attitude on the part of some of those who misunderstand and misinterpret some of Hartmann's proposals and aims. And there are some who feel that he interfered with their careers. If the Hartmann Era was so suppressing, if Kohut was heroic when he went against the Hartmannites, how do we understand the appearance, during the last thirty to forty years, of such a varied group of writers as those who characterize psychoanalytic discourse today?

An example of this kind of thinking in this book can be found in Bergmann›s opening appraisal of the Hartmann Era. Here he writes about Ernst Kris, whom he takes to be writing as though he were Hartmann, and his words, to Bergmann, seem as though they come from Hartmann. Bergmann describes twenty-one characteristic Hartmannite positions. "What makes the Hartmannites into a cohesive group are not only concepts and ideals they shared, but also a set of passionately held beliefs" (p. 9). Perhaps so, but the supposition of cohesiveness, I think, is largely in the eye of the beholder.

Bergmann writes of the Hartmannites that they passionately believed "Freud did not stop to systematize his findings .... Psychoanalysis is in dire need of systematization" (p. 9). "As [Ernst] Kris put it," Bergmann continues, "Sooner or later the ever more precise empirical test becomes an essential element in the development of any system of scientific propositions. In the development of psychoanalysis, this moment seems to have arrived" (p. 9).

Where is the logic here? This quotation fails to support Bergmann's proposal. There is no reference to systematization in this citation, despite the use of the word "system." Ernst Kris called for empirical tests to be applied to data. The Yale Study Group work; the work of Galenson and Roiphe; the refinement of psychological testing; the work of Stern outside the analytic consulting room; the current study of taped sessions; efforts to define the relation between analytic intervention, theories, and outcomes in the consulting room; and advances in brain science—all these share the same sense of necessity. Bergmann confuses *empirical research* with *systematization*.

It is clear that the demand for evidence and verifiability is seen as hostile by those who believe that what they impute to the infant's mind and then present as of primary significance to later development is truth, not hypothesis. Perhaps, since their ideas are beyond empirical proof and can never be verified, they seem to say, this demonstrates how profound that truth is. They believe they can know the primal by interpreting derivatives of derivatives in later mental life.

Apparently, some of us do not want to arrive at a system of scientific propositions based on data. Klein and Green, among others, have seen this as an inimical notion. Ironically, one of the explanations given at the conference, in seeking to explain why psychoanalysis has become less important in the community, is that we lack clear

196

evidence of the usefulness of analytic work, of the appropriateness of it in different cases, of the relation of theories to outcomes—a defect that they lay at the feet of the Hartmannites. But I suspect that Klein, Green, and others would not object to having empirical evidence that their approach leads to better results than someone else›s.

Green writes:

> I... wish to distinguish and even oppose what is "psychological" (meaning a general psychology that describes both health and pathology, and collects data subject to empirical test using a variety of approaches, and to keep it away from suppositions about the primacy of the Id, which is the basis and permanent determiner of human craziness, and unknowable in any case...), from what is "psychical." Space limitations do not allow me to justify this difference. [p. 115]

Most analysts passionately believe that their way of doing things is truer and more helpful for patients, while adhering to a system not based on empirical evidence or testing. So far, no one has shown by means of empirical evidence that his or her way is better than another. Nor has the power of various arguments deterred others from disagreeing, nor persuaded critics to revise their ideas. This leads me to another point made by some participants in the Hartmann Era conference, having to do with ego psychology's effect on analytic technique; a criticism was that the recommended clinical approaches led to longer and no more successful analyses, while making them more superficial.

Another criticism was that emphasis on the need for the analyst to remain anonymous led to the idealization of the analyst, encouraged the view of the analyst as powerful, and contributed to the analyst›s dominance over patients. These factors, putatively, led to later disappointment and depreciation of analysis. They also had institutional consequences—namely, in enhancing the authority of dominant practitioners, thereby supporting the stifling of independent thinking and challenge to the established analytic order.

Actually, Hartmann was fully aware of "the child's indomitable competitive urges for sexual gratification and narcissistic expansion. They induce wishful fantasies of sex, and sexual identification with aggrandized images of his love objects, predominantly of his admired preoedipal and oedipal rivals."[7] Note that Hartmann was aware of the importance of the preoedipal; note also that those who emphasize the importance of reality determinants of patients' behaviors are the same ones who decry Hartmann for an excessive emphasis on environmental context.

There are some comments in this book suggesting that Hartmann and his group were never as rigid as some of their followers were, and it seems evident that Hartmann, Bak, Ernst Kris, Marianne Kris, Bornstein, Loewenstein, Mahler, and Jacobson, to name a few, did not especially emphasize the need for anonymity. I once attended a dinner given by the Hartmanns at which my then-personal analyst was also an invitee. This event, along with impressions I formed of my analyst from his writings and his administrative and teaching interests, led to discussions we had in subsequent sessions. Through these, I came to conclude that my analyst was a somewhat moralistic man, but that that fact did not invalidate the conclusion that my anxiety about how much of a moralist and critic he might be, and how he could affect my career or livelihood, was largely a transference problem. Just because something is real does not make it less of a transference issue. It was quite useful to learn this.

---

7 Hartmann, H. (1964). *Ego Psychology and the Problem of Adaptation.* New York: Int. Univ. Press, p. 90.

Clinical discussions, supervision, and other instances at which case discussions took place revealed that quite a bit of self-revelation was common in these analysts' work with patients—directly, by way of offering examples cited from personal experience; by the use of jokes; by the offering of congratulations or regrets as appropriate situations arose. Certainly, students were asked to be careful and to remember that interventions were influenced by personal issues, and they were encouraged to take an analytic view of themselves and with their analysts. In that arena, countertransference was an accepted, inevitable factor, and the requirement that analytic students be in analysis while learning to do analysis was (and is) based on that understanding.

On the other hand, what used to be called *acting out* did take place. The Hartmann period, like others, was one of clique formation, the convoying of favorites by senior analysts, the splitting of institutes, and scandals about analysts› relations (and marriages) with patients. Perhaps these conditions were more prevalent, and/ or more threatening to psychoanalysis, than they are now. Probably, psychoanalytic officialdom was more rigid than now. The responsibility for overdone anonymity and the silence of some analysts; the unethical, impolite, and harmfully impetuous behaviors that took place then, earlier, and occur now; the personal arrogance; the petty rivalries; the blackballing of training analyst candidates—all these, nevertheless, can hardly be laid at the feet of Hartmann and his sympathizers, co-workers, and collaborators.

No one can predict what future generations will make of this book. Today's critics are making their contributions; those contributions will be digested and appropriated by others, and today's experts will inevitably become tomorrow's criticized—and then, largely, the next day's forgotten.

To sum up, I found large parts of the book lamentable. Some of the authors, including Grossman, Solnit, and Yorke, showed a clear understanding of Hartmann's work and times, but others displayed a lack of historical sophistication and an excess of ill-informed, ad hominem disparagement. The most interesting parts of the book were those in which the participants discussed their own ideas, which took place chiefly during the discussion period at the end of the conference.

CHAPTER 10

Unauthorized Freud. Doubters Confront a Legend

(1999). *Psychoanalytic Quarterly,* 68(2):330–334
Unauthorized Freud. Doubters Confront a Legend by
Frederick C. Crews, New York: Viking, 1998.331 pp.

There is much that usefully stimulates thought in Sills selection of brief statements by a number of critical Freud students who make points Crews agrees with and aims to promote.

In a necessarily brief review, it would be impossible to summarize and do justice to all that Crews presents here and all that he omits. He argues that Freud was a liar, seducer, bully, schemer, doer of vast harm, and all-around scoundrel who adopted a method he could use hypnotically and suggestively to impose his logically and scientifically unsupportable ideas on patients, whom he claimed to cure but failed to help. He plagiarized others' ideas. He was a bribing, threatening paternalist who created a squabbling, infantilized collection of damaged followers, who have failed, as Freud failed, to acknowledge their errors, apologize, and abandon their useless beliefs and practices. He created a false, self-aggrandizing personal myth of himself as a lonely, put-upon, unappreciated prophet. And he harmfully interfered in the lives of his patients; sometimes, as with Frink, the results were dire.

We can agree with Crews's list of some of Freud's more important errors. These include:

1. Freud claimed that he discovered that infantile seduction is the cause of neurosis and that he discovered the secret of dreams. Freud did not discover the source of the psychic Nile as he wished to. The Nile, in fact, has more than one source, and so do psychological phenomena.

2. The idea that recovery of the repressed memory of early traumatization brings about abreaction and cure is largely incorrect. To discuss traumatic experiences with another person, sometimes using hypnosis or drugs as an aid, can be very helpful, but a simple trauma-abreaction idea is insufficient.

3. That cure takes place through interpretation by an objective analyst who discovers important hidden contents simply by listening to the patient›s free associations is not accurate. In fact, the analyst pushes, interrupts, and educates patients by indicating what he wants to hear. Cure implies disease, and generally, analysts do not seek to cure diseases. This criticism is largely correct, though the effort to take this into account in the current practice of analytic work is omitted by Crews.

4. Freud's views that the oedipus complex is universal and psychologically central, and that penis envy is the main issue for women, are highly questionable. If as Crews does, one depends on a narrow definition of the oedipus complex, if repressed patricidal-sexual appropriation of the mother is defined as the oedipus complex, the idea is wrong. If that was Freud's idea, it was wrong. If neurosis is ascribed to this version of oedipus, that is wrong. The same goes for centrality of penis envy, which, incidentally, occurs in men as well as women. But Freud had a much more subtle view. He posited multiple (active, receptive, positive, negative, etc.) oedipal complexes.

5. That women are morally defective is clearly wrong.

6. That a patient's improvement demonstrates the correctness of the analyst's theory of cure is wrong. If two events coincide in time, one cannot logically be said to cause the other.

7. Freud did not always help his patients. But what alternative treatments were available? Those that were, when tried, hadn't helped.

8. Freud did at times behave unethically with patients. He failed to satisfy his, as well as our, standards.

9. The analytic method is imperfect and flawed since its propositions are not falsifiable. This is Grünbaum's, Popper's and Sidney Hook's argument, and it is true that no one can construct an experiment that will make falsifiability possible when it comes to psychoanalytic ideas. I once had dinner with Sidney Hook. When Hook learned I was an analyst, he asked me why and said that since analysts cannot imagine a person without an oedipus complex, one should not accept that there is such a thing. To know something requires seeing what would be there if the something were absent. I asked if Hook had a son. He did. Did he and the son have an amicable relationship? Not always, said Hook; they also competed with each other. Was Hook's relationship with this son quite like Mrs. Hook's relationship with him? No, the relationship between mother and son was different, more affectionate, and less competitive. Did Hook know any family where these things were absent? No, said Hook. That is an oedipus complex, said I. He'd have to think about it, said Hook. Nobody had put it just that way to him before.

Then this book criticizes contemporary psychoanalysis. "Contemporary analysts possess no reliable means, internal to 'clinical evidence,' of locating or correcting their own misconceptions" (p. x). True, but not entirely relevant. Analysts do not rely only on internal clinical evidence in arriving at or changing their conceptions and misconceptions. They also have other sources of information available to them. Clinical experiences, their own and those of others, child development observations, reports from parents in child analyses, clinical discussions with colleagues who may be treating relatives and friends of patients, reports from patients about the events and behavior of important people in their current lives, critiques of their work (as by Crews, et al.), all can enter into analysts› thinking. In addition, there is also the possibility that analysts learn something about their own tendencies toward certain misconceptions from their own analyses and from patients, readings, case discussions, and so on. Finally, psychoanalysis is the situation in which the interacting, wish-fear-influenced participants› interrelationship is an important subject for study.

We are told that "the emergence of latter day psychoanalytic incest inquisitors constitutes the most dramatic sign that the present book is neither antiquarian nor superfluous but urgently practical… every feature of recovered memory therapy, even the crudest, was pioneered by Freud, and nearly all those features were retained in his practice of psychoanalysis proper" (p. xi). Are incest inquisitors really psychoanalytic? Yes, says Borch-Jacobsen. He writes, "Are we much more advanced now that a hundred years have passed… Apparently not, to judge by the spectacular comeback of the traumatic-dissociative etiology of neurosis…" (p. 13). Are we analysts responsible for the practices of misusers, misstaters, and misunderstanders of "analytic" ideas? Are Borch-Jacobsen or Crews's colleagues responsible for such misstatements?

We also read that "free association proved every bit as contaminated as hypnosis had been…" (p. 5). Every bit?

Also, "Freud's Promethean self-analysis… was nothing more than a sequence of contradictory dreams and hallucinations that he

entertained and elaborated with cocaine-enhanced feverishness..."
(p. 7). Has Crews really read the Freud-Fliess letters? And what about
the Signorelli Parapraxis, the Disturbance of Memory paper, and
the Screen Memory paper, which together give a quite complicated
picture of Freud›s data and thinking about his psychology?

We are told that "Freudian dream theory has undergone little
alteration in nearly a century... REM sleep is universal among our
fellow mammals... none of whom is likely to be suffering from
repressed childhood memories or castration complexes..." (p. 73).
Actually, much has changed in regard to dream theory. By and
large, most psychoanalysts treat dreams like other psychological
phenomena, as examples of mental functioning to be understood
in terms of all that is known about the particular patient, including
what we know is not known, from the many available observations
of people in general. Dreams are probably not seen as the royal road
to the unconscious by most analysts. We do not use the topographic
model, with its important emphasis on the barriers between conscious
and unconscious and between latent and manifest much these days.
REM sleep may be universal among our fellow mammals, but highly
enlarged and developed cerebral cortexes, and their modifying
influences on subcortical activity, are not.

What Crews shows in this book is not only what he intends to
show about Freud and his faults, that analysts make questionable,
arguable assumptions, and that analysis is not an experimental or
mathematical study. He shows that good things can be misused, as
Freud and other analysts can misuse their patients and their method
and as Crews and some of his included authors do, in purveying
misinformation, prejudices, and hostility under the guise of presenting
logical, historically accurate, supposedly factual information.

There are better and worse psychoanalysts, and better and
worse critics and historians. Crews shows something important by

example as well as by demonstration and argument. That is, in the study of complex systems, like the functioning of a particular mind, the interrelationships between people, or the history of personal or societal development, no available methodology can eliminate the fact that logic, observation, and the selection of data can be used and, probably inevitably, are used to serve the wishes, defenses, moralities, and adaptational possibilities of authors. No method can entirely eliminate the possibility of people causing harm in their writings and teachings.

This volume provides a guided tour, a Crews-led cruise, through the ideascapes of writings of eighteen Freud critics, whose views he shares. These are some well-known figures, like Peter J. Swales, Frank J. Sulloway, Adolf Grünbaum, Joseph Wolpe, Stanley Fish, some less well known writers and, most importantly, Crews himself, who Chapter 11 uses the selections to speak for him, and tells us what they say. If taking Freud and his work seriously and as important enough to consider critically is a compliment, then this book is complimentary to that extent. Because critical views of ideas expressed by intelligent authors give those holding the criticized ideas a possibility of rethinking and then of modifying or abandoning their ideas, this book presents psychoanalysts with an unusual, concise opportunity to reconsider those ideas.

The book presents interesting views in a trenchant, relentless, stylish, and often amusing manner. Less positively, the tone is often outrageously provocative or exaggerated, and the critiques can be smugly insistent, as though there is nothing else to be said. This quality lessens the force of some arguments, especially when what is being criticized about Freud is his un-self-questioning infatuation with his own ideas, his lack of respect for others' views, and his hectoring, bullying manner. Of course, this take-no-prisoners, polemic approach also provides an amusing read.

More negatively, there are important instances when a seeming absence of scholarship, knowledge, and understanding is evident, and this permits oversimplified or plainly wrong conclusions to be proposed. Arguments that Freud failed to do his homework, as in the Leonardo paper, and that he impulsively jumped to conclusions are weakened when the critics misbehave similarly. Further still into negative territory are some patently false statements. All in all, however, we and our patients owe Crews a vote of thanks for this presentation.

CHAPTER 11.

Freud, Dora, and Vienna, 1900

994). *Journal of the American Psychoanalytic Association,* 42:894–898
Freud, Dora, and Vienna, 1900: by Hannah S. Decker.
New York: Free Press, 1991, 229 pp., $22.95.

Decker's researches provide a great deal of information, much of it new, about Ida Bauer (Dora), her family, and their friends the Zellenka (K.) family, and she describes and discusses aspects of the social and cultural milieu in which they lived. Decker also proposes that societal misogyny and anti-Semitism had important effects on Ida Bauer's personal development, discusses aspects of psychoanalysis by, and since, Freud, and evaluates Freud's work in the Dora case. Decker thus emphasizes social influences in the Dora case rather than the intrapsychic and family-oriented approach that has usually been of most interest to analysts.

Analysts have valued the paper which came to be known as the Dora case for several reasons, but the main ones are that in it Freud (1905) enunciated some basic discoveries. He proposed that symptoms "represent several processes simultaneously" and have more than one meaning (p. 47). A second point was, "The causes of hysterical disorders are to be found in the intimacies of the patient's psychosexual life and are the expression of their most secret and repressed wishes" (p. 12), a third: dream interpretation is woven into the history of the treatment and "can become the means of filling in amnesias and elucidating symptoms" (p. 10).

Other of Freud's ideas of this time have been accepted as wrong. Freud thought masturbating caused leukorrhea, and that a syphillitic parent transmitted a hereditary taint to offspring. He thought successful treatment depended on the respect and admiration the patient had for the doctor, and he behaved in an authoritarian and directing way toward patients.

Freud's and Ida Bauer's paths crossed during an active period in Freud's analytic development, long before analysts had developed the still incomplete understanding of psychology with which we now look back to those days almost a century ago.

No doubt, the combination of Freud's remarkable ideas, his clinical ingenuity, the unraveling of a mystery, the enticing interrelationships among the personalities involved in Ida Bauer's life, and the incompleteness of Freud's understanding of his own and her psychology, have all contributed to the interest this case study has aroused. Milton Horowitz counted, and informs me that over 350 published contributions have taken up the case, reanalyzed the patient, and critiqued Freud's understanding and handling of it.

Decker's book is a serious effort, and well worth reading for the information it provides and for the critique it stimulates. There are, of course, weaknesses as well as strengths in this contribution. On the positive side, Decker adds to our knowledge of the personal conditions of the patient's life. The additions in this sphere will be of great interest to psychoanalysts. She also argues for an expanded appreciation of the important influence social context has on individual development and adaptation, since the community offers opportunities and for gratification and fitting in, as well as obstacles. Decker emphasizes the special restrictions Ida Bauer faced as a woman and as a Jew. The contrast in the restrictions and demands on her as she grew up with those that affected her later famous, political leader brother Otto, is especially telling.

An interesting discussion of electrotherapy as used at the time, and applied in Ida. Bauer's case, suggests that experiences with doctors who applied this painful and unsuccessful treatment probably facilitated the displacement of her ambivalent attitude about authorities to Freud. K. R. Eissler's (1986) volume, *Freud as an Expert Witness*, presents Freud's later (1920) views about the more or less cruel use of electrotherapy for treating war neuroses and gives some comparisons of malingering and hysteria that would be appropriate comparative reading.

Decker describes the changing legal, economic, and social situation of Bohemian and Viennese Jews. Here, specific information about the Bauers is sparse, and she relies on general history, diaries, and individual opinions to support her ideas about what influenced Ida Bauer. For example, quotations from Arthur Schnitzler and Karl Kraus are taken as representative of typical experience and opinion, and are too directly applied to Ida Bauer's situation. Decker explains Jews' conversions to Christianity, assimilationism, and prejudices among older established Jews against more recent arrivals by means of "Jewish-self-hatred," and supposes that because this self-hatred was so prevalent, it must have affected Ida Bauer too, and been one of her main problems: At the end of the century, "Jews began to blame each other for the anti-Semitism that surrounded them. Assimilated Jews blamed Eastern Jews and vice versa. Intellectual Jews were embarrassed by both. Modern Jewish self-hatred raged" (p. 37). Decker proposes that Ida Bauer's neurotic behavior was caused dominantly by these social experiences of late adolescence.

There are several difficulties her argument does not resolve. How representative of Ida Bauer's context are the contemporaneous opinions Decker adduces? Are all assimilations, conversions, and prejudices among Jews to be accounted for in the same way? Do ambition, adaptation, the idiosyncratic personal experiences of childhood before adolescence, the particular capacities for synthesis and originality, among others, enter into "Jewish self-hatred," and if so, how?

Even if direct evidence of Ida Bauer's experiencing anti-Semitism and its effect on her could have been adduced, the period of her childhood, before her family's return to Vienna, was one in which restriction was undergoing modification. Liberalization and opportunity for women and Jews as well were expanding. Ida Bauer's societal life was privileged and protected, and not the life of a typical Jewish woman. What was the psychological effect of these aspects of the social context? What was the effect of the changes in the social fabric that occurred later in Ida's life, given what she experienced earlier?

What was the significance of factors, likely important, that had not changed, not emphasized by Decker? At the time, contraception was unreliable. Illegitimacy was common. Communicable diseases, including sexually transmitted diseases, were rampant and mostly untreatable. People married for dynastic reasons and had extramarital affairs, more or less openly. These conditions had consequences for everyone, including the Bauers.

If not all possible social influences are emphasized by Decker, some idiosyncratic family factors seem neglected in her discussion. Not many Jewish fathers were as rich and entrepreneurial as Philipp Bauer. Not many women were neurotically afflicted as was Dora-Ida's mother. Not many tubercular fathers retired to the mountains with their families for years. How many were hypocritical as Philipp was? Schnitzler claimed to "portray the reality that underlay upright, bourgeois existence" (p. 109). If Philipp was a common type of father, how significant was it that his type was common and how significant that he was Ida's father?

The proposition that social context is important, and too often neglected, is unarguable. Social attitudes and conditions produce important experiences whose effects are transmitted through generations. Decker's argument will seem a comfortable friend to analytic readers. Heinz Hartmann, as an example, clearly described how individuals create communities and construct institutions as vehicles for gratification and to aid them in controlling and punishing their own impulses, and *per contra*, how such institutions impose restrictions and distortions.

Perhaps the most unfortunate aspect of the book is Decker's reanalysis of Freud's analysis of Dora. Preconceptions and a political agenda seem to inform an unbalanced approach that results, in my view, in too much critique based on hindsight, and too little description of how analysis evolved out of nineteenth-century psychiatry, Austria out of the remains of the Holy Roman Empire, and 1990's attitudes about social life out of the hierarchic familial forms of the 1890's. If Ida Bauer is to be seen in her social historical context, science should be too.

Decker writes, "What had gone wrong?" in the Dora case. She answers, "As diverse as the causes of Dora's hysteria was the baggage—personal as well as professional—that the middle-aged Freud brought to a seemingly straightforward case" (p. 2). "At no time in his career was Freud prepared to recognize women's sensibilities" (p. 107).

In her conclusion, Decker states "Freud's psychoanalysis of Dora... does not yield a totally black picture..." Decker estimates that Freud "did help Dora." Nevertheless, "the psychoanalysis did Dora permanent harm. Freud compounded her father's betrayal by his unconscious exploitation of her. His primary interest in her predicament lay in using her psychoanalysis to support his theories and his reputation; his interest in curing her, though real, was secondary. Furthermore, Freud's sexual intrusion [Decker means his sexual interpretations and authoritarian attitude], although again unconscious, mimicked only too well Mr. K.'s and her father's. To whatever extent Dora had come to believe that the adult world was manipulative and scheming before she got onto Freud's couch, the analysis helped to solidify her view" (pp. 198–199).

As to references to support these views: Decker cites Peter Swales, an enthusiastic Freud critic, to corroborate her own critical views, and misuses the work of Theodore Jacobs (whose purpose is to show how the analyst can use self-evaluation to forward analyses) to show that, even today, analysts are troubled about harmful countertransferences. She does not refer to Heinz Hartmann, Ernst Kris, Rudolph M. Loewenstein, Sandor Ferenczi, Robert Waelder, Melanie Klein, Karen Horney, Heinz Kohut, and D. W. Winnicott, to say nothing of Charles Brenner and Jacob A. Arlow. The retrospectoscope through which she evaluates her evidence is missing some important lenses.

In conclusion: I recommend this book to analytic readers. It brings forward new data; retells much that is of historical interest; unfortunately, leaves out mention of other significant factors; and reveals the influence of current understanding of the harmful effects of mysogyny and prejudice—a point of view deserving of attention, even though here somewhat overenthusiastically presented.

REFERENCES

Eissler, K.R. (1986). *Freud as an Expert Witness*. Madison, CT: Int. Univ. Press.

Freud, S. (1905). Fragment of an analysis of a case of hysteria *S.E. 7*.

——— (1920). Memorandum on the electrical treatment of war neurotics *S.E. 1*,

CHAPTER 12

Freud for Historians

987). *Psychoanalytic Quarterly,* 56:402–403.
Freud for Historians by Peter Gay. New York/Oxford:
Oxford University Press, 1985. 252 pp.

There are at least three main aspects to this book. It is a psychoanalytic primer intended for the edification of historians. As such, it presents mainstream psychoanalytic views succinctly and pleasingly, in relatively jargon-free, straightforward language. Secondly, the book serves as a vessel to contain reviews and asides that comment on the work of many authors, both historians and psychoanalysts. Gay's comments, some brief and some more extended, include appreciations, chidings, analyses, and suggestions. Some are stimulating and very worthwhile; all are of interest. Thirdly, the book raises a number of questions of general intellectual interest, often without providing answers.

Gay discusses the tendency of many historians towards reductionistic thinking. They prefer to limit their view of motivation to self-interest in a narrow sense, omitting consideration of such factors as sexuality, aggression, guilt, and defensive trends. Analysts, on the other hand, and Gay quotes Hartmann in support of his point, often omit self-interest from their consideration, and they neglect practical, realistic factors in their historical explanations. Analysts could perform a very useful function if they were to contribute an understanding of how libidinal, aggressive, moral, and defensive wishes interrelate with contextual, historic reality. Such a contribution would help historians to enlarge their view of self-interest and of conflicts among multiple interests. Gay chides analysts who fail to provide connections between such "hard realities" as food scarcities and technical innovations, conflicts in which the mind clearly has an important share, such as class antagonisms, and the "murky underworld of the concealed and contradictory emotions that are the psychoanalyst's chosen playground" (p. 119). Neither the rational nor the irrational, neither fantasy nor the real, should be slighted.

Gay proposes a second problem issue. This relates to the understanding of the connections between individual biography and group behavior. He believes insufficient work has been done in furthering the understanding of interrelationships between crowd psychology and the functioning of institutions and individual psychology, between what he calls "the stubborn self" and "indispensable and stifling culture."

Gay's predominant message as revealed in this book is his belief that historical and psychoanalytic understanding can and should further develop interconnections that have, until now, been only indicated. He commends the work of Crews and Hawthorne on Woodrow Wilson, and Demos on Salem witchcraft, among others, as pioneering efforts tending in what he sees as a desirable progress toward "total history."

The book is urbane and wide-ranging. It reflects an interesting and educated mind, and reading it is certain to be rewarding to those with even a modest interest in the subject.

CHAPTER 13

Freud in Germany. Revolution and Reaction in Science, 1893–1907

(1985). *Journal of the American Psychoanalytic Association* 33:702–706.
*Freud in Germany. Revolution and Reaction in Science,
1893-1907.* Psychological Issues, Monogr. 41 by Hannah
S. Decker. New York: International Universities Press,
1977, xi + 364 pp., $28.50 (soft cover, $22.50).

Decker's book has two purposes. One is historical, the second, critical. As to the historical aspect, Decker describes Freud's early ideas, the situation of the German culture and society, and the psychological, psychiatric, and politico-social thought of the period 1893-1907 in order to examine the German response to early psychoanalysis. The second purpose is to show that Freud's often stated opinion that he was ignored, unappreciated, or reviled at that time was historically inaccurate and that in fact, his writings were read, seriously discussed, and influential. The historical information she gives has a value for those interested in the evolution of psychoanalytic ideas. The political, critical use to which Decker puts the information she presents, to fault Freud, to reveal him as a neurotic, will have a value to those who, while they may or may not be interested in the development of psychoanalysis, have some desire to diminish Freud.

Freud is generally regarded as one of the towering discoverers, revolutionaries, and creators of history. He associated himself with heroic peers: biblical figures such as Joseph and Moses, and historic ones such as Plato and Leonardo. He wrote of them as a colleague would, as forebears, rivals, and human beings resembling himself. He speculated about their personal psychologies as he investigated his own. Freud had Promethean ambitions.

At the same time, Freud repeatedly asserted he was unappreciated, reviled, and, at a brilliant period in his career, isolated. Such opinions can be found in "An Autobiographical Study," in the paper on "The Resistances to Psycho-analysis," in letters and other writings. He explained this "response" to his work as motivated by resistance to the new, by «social hypocrisy» which increased antipathy to instinctual expression, and by the force of neurotic resistances and anti-Semitism in his audience. In describing himself as isolated and unappreciated, Freud portrayed himself as similar to his heroes. He was intellectually parentless. He gave birth to his new science, alone. Rank described this fantasy in *The Myth of the Birth of the Hero*. Freud directly emphasized his resemblance to Moses. The seduction theory was the discovery of the «caput Nili.» In discovering penis envy he had discovered the «bedrock of neurosis." In dreams he appeared as Joseph. Freud›s attitude about himself and his place in history was created in part out of wishes motivated by unconscious forces and conflicts, as he was the first to say. In part, it was profoundly based on verifiable data. Freud the historian knew he was a man. In his historical interests, he gratified the patricidal wishes and filial love that he discovered in himself and in others, and that he wished to reveal to us all.

If Freud wished to believe that Shakespeare should not be credited with the authorship of *Hamlet*, some living historians wish to show that Freud was not Freud. They say: he was not a perfect original, but a man of his time; his efforts to gain acceptance for his ideas were not absolutely constructive; and most particularly, his work did evoke positive responses during the period of «isolation." Further, to the extent that he was opposed, opposition was motivated by factors other than those he suggested. Freud was a neurotic.

These are the points Decker, the author of this book, makes and supports, with much convincing evidence. Freud was not Freud, or at least not the Freud he probably wished to be or the Freud some wish he had been. Ernest Jones, among other followers, is specifically criticized because he accepted some of Freud's statements about himself. Making these points may be worthwhile even to a psychoanalytic readership, or perhaps not.

The author writes (p. 2), "... the reasons why psychoanalysis ultimately failed to make a significant impression in German professional circles are manifold and extend beyond the usually repeated trio of sexual prejudice, anti-Semitism and the critic›s personal neurosis." She wishes to add, as a cause, the criticized's personal neurosis. The author fails to tell us what she means by "ultimate" or "significant" or to admit that these terms reflect her personal preferences. She depreciates Freud. In "An Autobiographical Study," in "The Resistance to Psycho-analysis," and in the "Address to the Society of B'nai B'rith," he gave explanations far beyond the usual trio.

In the course of our analytic historical investigations of ourselves and our patients, we have learned that historical research can gratify desires to idealize, to be close to and retain our progenitors, and to dethrone and supplant them. Often enough, conflicts involving such desires limit our successes. Decker demonstrates that in Germany in his period, Freud was read, reviewed, discussed, to a degree understood and appreciated. He was not entirely alone or rejected. Decker's reader is led to the inevitable conclusion that Freud exaggerated. His statements that he was neglected, or at best, only reviled, were wrong. The psychoanalyst might take the demonstration of Freud's subjectivity as inevitable, and as an historical phenomenon

219

to be historically explained, but Decker does not. She regards her conclusion as a worthwhile discovery in itself.

To those for whom this conclusion is foregone, the discovery is of little interest. What is of interest is what the historical data suggest. Decker recreates the theater of scientific controversy of the time. With the benefit of hindsight, we can more clearly confront the ingenious discoveries Freud made and the unsolved questions, some not answered even yet, that his investigations forced on his contemporaries, and to a degree on us, his heirs and successors. We can wonder that some ideas like abreaction theory, to us incomplete, were largely accepted and that some, like the discovery of the importance of infantile sexuality, now largely accepted, were opposed. Most significantly, we can acknowledge, because of the clarity distance increases, difficulties present then and with us now.

Some of these difficulties have to do with scientific problems, some with the human problems, overenthusiasm and overambition. Both are displayed in the panorama Decker presents.

In the scientific area, there were and are problems of integrating materials derived from differing approaches. These included and include anatomical, chemical-physical and genetic approaches. Late nineteenth-century German "scientific" psychiatry was dominated by brain psychiatrists who espoused a materialistic and mechanistic medicine as exemplified by Meynert's 1892 *Clinical Diseases of the Forebrain*. This approach was supported by the discoveries of brain localization, the neurone and the relation between syphilis and general paresis.

Other approaches to the understanding of the human animal that were not integrated were clinical-psychiatric. These efforts to classify ailments by describing syndromes according to manifest symptomatology and course (Kraepelin, for example) went on then, as now. Then, as now, integrations and harmonizations of the different approaches were elusive. Decker's statement, "There was scant awareness of the ill person as a whole being, made up of highly complex, interacting physical and psychological systems," makes the point that even now, the author, a rather knowing person, can pass over the philosophical and diagnostic problems connected with the decision about what is ill and what is healthy (what is a hysteric, what a hysteric symptom), to go on to the paradoxical assertion that a whole being is made up of interacting separable systems, all the while assuming an air of superior wisdom in comparison with the befuddlements of the past. Those of the Kraepelinian persuasion, to whom mental disease and mental health were not relative states, and to whom there was no continuum between the two are epigones to many of us who wonder how extensive relativism may be. Mind-body and illness-health dualistic thinking persists among analysts as well as among *DSM-III* psychiatrists and historians. We have not yet arrived at a whole elephant. And even the monists among us know that we remain largely ignorant about the specifics of quantities of the nature-nurture contributions, the «complementary series,» to the conditions we observe in individual cases.

Even those who approached mental material from an approach similar to Freud›s objected that Freud went too far in attributing all psychopathology to repression of memories of infantile sexual impressions (e.g., E. Bleuler). Their views were shared by later Freudians, and the later Freud. Their objections were answered by later developments—the understanding of the role of aggression, and of the importance of the development of object relations, as examples. Those who objected that creative achievement represented more than sublimation of sexual wishes (e.g., Kraepelin) were followed by authors who emphasized the importance of the biologically given evolving ego capacities. The question, why is symptom formation attributed to such an extent to oedipal factors, when traumatic neurosis can be observed to bring on symptoms (e.g., W. H. Hellpach), and when symptoms can precede the oedipal period, was raised by Freud›s opponents and later by Freud and his associates.

As to the matter of overenthusiasm, Freud's early attitude that sexual matters dominate symptomatology, later that penis

ainting ourselves with the intricacies of the discoveries and enthusiasms of that historic period, will inform us and represent for our consideration some of the considerable scientific problems we still face. Perhaps, in addition, it will remind us that enthusiasm also has its destructive side.

CHAPTER 14

Psychoanalytic Research. Three Approaches to the Experimental Study of Subliminal Processes

(1976). *Psychoanalytic Quarterly*, 45:321–323
*Psychoanalytic Research. Three Approaches to the Experimental Study of Subliminal Processes edited by Martin Mayman.
Psychological Issues*, Vol. VIII, No. 2, Monograph 30. New York: International Universities Press, Inc., 1973. 135 pp.

This publication is an expanded version of a 1966 American Psychological Association Symposium. It includes three experimental and two philosophical papers dealing with problems of methodology, relevance, and soundness. Mayman provides a brief historical survey of psychoanalytically related research, and some explanation of the importance of experimentation as a means of hypothesis testing, discovering new data, and developing theory.

Donald P. Spence and Carol M. Gordon, in *Activation and Assessment of an Early Oral Fantasy: an Exploratory Study,* describe their studies of the effect of the interplay of rejection, characterologic orality, and subliminal stimulation on subjects' recall of word lists and their importation of falsely recollected words. Characterologically oral individuals responded to the combination of rejection and subliminal exposure of the word 'milk' by importing regressive oral words (milk, bottle, nipple, etc.) when asked to recall a word list, and by tending to recall the more infantile words on the list (suck, mother, formula).

The bias toward infantile food words is taken as supporting the idea that an organized unconscious fantasy is activated by rejection, and its influence emerges in verbal recall if an ‹associative network› is activated by a mediating subliminal stimulus.

In an article, *Forgetting and Remembering (Momentary Forgetting) During Psychotherapy: a New Sample,* Lester Luborsky summarizes and adds to earlier publications that examine the clinical situation in which a patient realizes he has forgotten a thought, pauses to try to recover it, and then either remembers or gives up the search. This phenomenon, naturalistically studied in its clinical context, occurs in a ‹distracted state› involving near-forgetting, uncertainty about the thoughts, and confusion about expressing them. The forgetting, which usually occurs only after twenty minutes of a session have passed, is preceded by explicit references to the therapist. At this point, the patient feels rejected, and the patient's material reflects a theme specific for that patient. Luborsky points to the obvious relevance of this data to the understanding of anxiety, transference, repression, etc.

Howard Shevrin, in *Brain Wave Correlates of Subliminal Stimulation, Unconscious Attention, Primary—and Secondary— Process Thinking, and Repressiveness,* describes a series of experimental studies. Using a drawing composed of a pen and a knee as a stimulus, he found that conceptual (e.g., ink to pen, calf to knee) associations resulted from supraliminal presentation, and rebus (coin to pen-knee) associations from subliminal presentation. Subjects exposed to subliminal presentation of the drawing gave rebus associations when awakened from REM sleep, conceptual associations when awakened from NREM sleep. Further work involved using Average Cortical Evoked Responses (AER) as derived from mathematical averaging of EEG responses. The AER was different when subjects directed their attention outward to a tactile stimulus, consciously inward (mental arithmetic), unconsciously inward in associating to a subliminal presentation, and unconsciously inward when they associated freely (resulting in alpha rhythm). Character type as measured by psychological assessment of regressiveness also influences the quantity of conceptual and rebus associations as well as correlated AER patterns. The author suggests that two processes of deployment of attention operate: in the unconscious process of ‹repression›, attention can be withdrawn from inner stimuli; in the conscious process of ‹avoidance› it can be focused on neutral external stimuli. One or both processes are active in defense.

Philip S. Holzman in *Some Difficulties in the Way of Psychoanalytic Research: a Survey and a Critique* emphasizes that analytic theory is an unsystematized collection of 'microtheories... loosely tied together', that academically trained psychologists often have insufficient clinical training to do research, that institute-trained clinicians know too little 'science', and that psychoanalytic research is conceived of too narrowly. He recommends that questions should range from those about therapeutic efficacy to those about specific functions (memory, perception), and that investigators should have a sophisticated clinical and scientific background.

Paul E. Meehl concludes the volume with a plea for avoiding extremes both of empiricism and relativistic antiempiricism.

Brief summaries cannot do justice to the thoughtful well-integrated papers, based on years of consideration and experimentation, that the authors have contributed to this small volume. Shevrin's chapter is particularly rich both in data and thought and will interest the most clinically minded, as well as the experimentally oriented reader. But the other authors, particularly in the investigative papers, offer food for thought as well. The comments of Mayman, Holzman, and Meehl attempt to justify a point of view to an audience made up of psychologists. These are historically and philosophically cursory, and will be of less interest to analysts.

225

A surprising omission in a book concerned with problems of psychoanalytic theory and evidence is any sign of indebtedness or even reference to the work of Heinz Hartmann. Had he written only *Die Grundlagen der Psychoanalyse,* he should be recognized as a scientific grandfather of the present volume.

CHAPTER 15

Shorter Book Reviews

(1975). *Psychoanalytic Review.* LXI, 1974: *Sleep and Dreams in the Analytic Hour: The Analysis of an Obsessional Patient.* Lillian H. Robinson. pp. 115–131. *Psychoanalytic Quarterly,* 44:495.

After a review of some of the clinical literature on sleep during the analytic hour, the author presents the case of a patient who had a number of sleep episodes during analytic sessions. She demonstrates the complexity in the various aspects of the structure of this symptom in relation to the transference and genetic factors. These include confusion and admixture of feelings of anger, fear, and sexual excitement, as well as defensive and wishful elements.

(1975). *Psychoanalytic Review.* LX, 1973: The 'As If' Personality and Transvestitism. Michael A. Sperber. pp. 605-612. *Psychoanalytic Quarterly,* 44:172.

A case of transvestitism is presented. The patient is seen as an 'as if' personality who, because of preoedipal disappointment with objects, is limited to imitation of them. He dresses like his mother but does not identify with her in her choice of sexual object, as a homosexual or transsexual would.

(1974). *Psychoanalytic Review*. LIX, 1972: Psychoanalysis and History: Problems and Applications. Joseph A. Dowling. pp. 433–449. *Psychoanalytic Quarterly*, 43:156.

American reform movements have shared a millenialistic air. Populism, for example, looked back to an agrarian Eden in looking forward to social reforms. The belief in a lost paradise and the wish to re-create it, which are applied in efforts to deal with objective problems of the day, derive from subjective experiences of satisfaction in early childhood.

(1973). *Psychoanalytic Review*. LVIII, 1971: *Incest and Culture: A Reflection on Claude Lévi-Strauss* by Richard Scheckner. pp. 562–572. *Psychoanalytic Quarterly*, 42:160.

Lévi-Strauss defines and distinguishes between nature and culture. Marriage rules establish culture by creating social organization based on exchanges of women. The incest prohibition affirms ‹the pre-eminence of the social over the natural› (i.e., over incestuous wishes), and is the most focused part of the social systems of exchange. Marriage and initiations resolve the parent›s as well as the child›s incestuous problems. The child passes from the parent to the social orbit; in return, the parent is entitled to someone else›s child.

(1972). *Psychoanalytic Review.* LVIII, 1971: Dependency Conflicts in the Young Adult. Joseph Barnett. Pp. 111–125. *Psychoanalytic Quarterly,* 41:306–306.

The author states that 'the cognitive matrix' of the child entering adolescence ‹is largely structured by... the implicit family ideology›. Adolescence, bringing new capacities for cognition and a larger social environment, presents a creative task: to restructure and comprehend experience, and develop patterns of 'intimacy and effort'. Anxiety results from ‹confrontation with chaos› and is alleviated by regression to dependency on the family or on an alternate ideology.

(1972). *Psychoanalytic Review.* LVII, 1970: *Self-Reconstitution Processes A Preliminary Report* by Theodore R. Sarbin and Nathan Adler. Pp. 599–616. *Psychoanalytic Quarterly,* 41:152.

A number of elements are common to 'self-reconstitution processes' such as religious conversion, brainwashing, Synanon and Alcoholics Anonymous experiences, psychotherapy, military indoctrination, and hypnosis. These elements include symbolic death and rebirth, a relationship with a group and its esteemed representative (teacher, oracle), ritual behavior that allows the acolyte an active role, special bodily stimuli (kneeling, lying, hunger, etc.), and ‹triggers›, which are special events that stimulate conversion. Such conversion procedures involve ‹a physical and psychological assault (symbolic death); a developing confusion about self and other beliefs... surrender and despair (becoming a nonperson) and... a working through, active mastery, re-education or adaptation process (the rebirth experience)'.

(1970). *The Nature of the Creative Process in Art. A Psychological Study* By Jaroslav Havelka. The Hague: Martinus Nijhoff, 1968. 230 pp. *Psychoanalytic Quarterly, 39:495–497*

Professor Havelka suggests a theory of the nature of creativity which includes ‹complex associated mental processes, subjective psychic dispositions, and cognitive intentions› and is built upon 'what is implicit in Freud'. The basis for his theory lies in the primary processes, 'the primitive conditions of some of which can eventually be detected as originating in neural and psychological functions'. He mistakenly attacks what he says is Freud's idea that creativity is merely resolution of neurosis through sublimation.[8] Havelka understands creativity in terms of symbolic mental structure, imagination and stylistic form resulting from interactions between conscious, preconscious and unconscious' which 'determine the primitive constituents of the creative act and expression'. These constituents, activated by 'comic intention', a quality of mental tension accompanied by a tendency toward economy of mental expenditure, or by 'tragic intention', a quality of mental tension relating to the reaction of fright in association with the uncanny, produce the creative act.

In a parsimonious way, the creative act, according to Havelka, integrates uncommunicable mental events, consciousness, present and past, archaic elements of mental formation, and present expression into an ambiguous symbolic structure that may be contemplated. The receiving mind opens ‹cyclical oscillations› and ‹expansions› that follow the artist›s mental rhythm. Imagination is the function that reduces ‹multitude into unity of effect›. A spiritual canticle of

---

8 In 1933, in a preface to Marie Bonaparte's The Life and Works of Edgar Allen Poe, Freud wrote: 'Investigations of this kind are not intended to explain an author's genius, but they show what motive forces aroused it and what material was offered to him by destiny›.

St. John of the Cross is given as an example: ‹all that is fearful and all that is blissful merges into one expression of subjective ambiguity, and thereby a mental closure is achieved where a creative expression mitigates the opposites and formally determines the unlimited significance of the imaginative reality of faith.' Pleasure in this creation is experienced because primitive drives are asserted, energy is saved, closure is achieved, while ambiguity is retained.

Havelka's range of interests is wide, and stimulating. He discusses myth and Oedipus, Picasso and Matisse, regression and play, Hebb, Piaget, etc. Often his ideas are controversial or unsubstantiated. For instance, he writes that in the adolescent period ‹too much concentrated effort is spent... in consolidating the ongoing learning processes so that they will fit into the collective patterning of reactions, and comparatively little energy is invested in the preservation of continuity between the primary and secondary functions›. And, ‹When one becomes tired because of fatigue products and certain glandular secretions a conflict arises between the sleep-producing and sleep-repressing mechanisms. The resolution of this conflict is sleep itself accompanied by a quality of pleasure... which stems primarily from the resolution of the above-mentioned conflict.'

The author's tendentiousness about Freud (who has 'notions' while other writers have 'ideas') is sometimes irritating. One wishes Havelka had more understanding of Freud's works and the writings of more recent authors such as Waelder, Lewin, Hartmann, Kris, and Loewenstein. Havelka's theory does not include the questions of ontogenesis, or the specific intrapsychic, and external conditions that evoke a creative act, of especial interest to psychoanalysis. However, certain of his ideas are subtle and important and the book is an interesting and stimulating contribution to the literature on the relation of art, æsthetics, and *psychology.*

(1971). *Psychoanalytic Review.* .LVII, 1970: *Freud, Leonardo and the Lamb.* Durward J. Markle, Jr. Pp. 285–288. *Psychoanalytic Quarterly,* 40:376.

Markle finds that the child in the Holy Family of da Vinci is releasing rage on the lamb in the picture. The lamb is tense and unbalanced because of the child's grip on its neck. Perhaps the picture portrays da Vinci as the child expressing his rage at his abandonment by his mother at age five. Freud's suggestion that this painting shows a blissful scene underemphasizes his observation that the lamb was ‹maltreated›.

www.ingramcontent.com/pod-product-compliance
Lightning Source LLC
Chambersburg PA
CBHW062127020426
42335CB00013B/1125